BIKE FOR BURUNDI

BIKE FOR BURUNDI

A RIDE ACROSS ONE COUNTRY
FOR THE FUTURE OF ANOTHER

SIMON GUILLEBAUD

Charleston, South Carolina

BIKE FOR BURUNDI

A Ride Across One Country
For The Future Of Another

Published by Four Winds Books
PO Box 21597
Charleston, SC 29413
www.FourWindsBooks.org

The names and identifying details of some
characters in this book have been changed.

For information about discounts for bulk purchases,
please contact Four Winds Books Special Sales:
(843) 323-6822 or sales@fourwindsbooks.org

To schedule a speaking engagement, Simon can be contacted at:
www.simonguillebaud.com

ISBN 978-0-9854127-3-9

Printed in the United States of America
First Edition 2012

To Geoff Morris...

A great man, with shared tears at how it panned out for you. But the whole thing was your idea and so many lives will be impacted as a result. Thanks mate! And to Michelle, because behind every great man...is a woman rolling her eyes!

CONTENTS

PROLOGUE

Muslims claim that Mohammed, the founder of their religion, entered a trance-like state in order to receive the sublime words of the Koran by divine revelation, as Allah dictated them to him in perfect Arabic.

I claim no divine revelation for this work, no new religion, and no beautifully-crafted language. But much of it was written in a not dissimilar trance-like state! The following pages first appeared as a blog, mostly written in a semi-comatose state in the back of a smelly, cramped RV in the late (or early) hours at one end or another of yet another gruelling day of cycling across the massive expanse of America.

During the course of this adventure, I was cursed (or blessed, I guess, since that's how the blog came into being) with being a terrible sleeper. Sleep is critical in any endurance event to recharge your batteries—but I generally found it impossible to quickly nod off. So I begrudgingly used that time to record what happened on our crazy adventure. Within a few days of posting the first blog, people were writing back to me, telling me it had to become a book. The blog went viral and the rest is history.

So please enjoy our sufferings vicariously and I hope they provide some chuckles along the way.

INTRODUCTION

"I teach people to shag."

Bear with me. You have to understand the context. I had just given a talk to a sophisticated, high-society group of "mature" ladies at St Michael's Episcopal Church in Charleston, South Carolina. I'd been sharing about my missionary work with pygmies and orphans in Burundi, Central Africa. I'd also discussed my impending cycle trip across the USA from the West to East coast to raise money for those projects. Apparently, the talk had gone well. We'd closed the meeting, and now I was sitting next to a 70-year-old, well-dressed lady with a twinkle in her eye. My question had been a normal one ("What do you do?"). Her answer had not!

"Sorry, could you say that again?"

"I teach people to shag."

She looked great for her age, and I could see that in her heyday she would have been a real corker. Indeed, she seemed like an upstanding and respectable member of the community. So her words pricked my ears all the more. What did she mean?

A few years before my family and I did so, a Scottish minister friend of mine had also moved to Charleston. As he was being shown around his new home by a friendly lady member of his congregation, she'd stunned him with a similar question: "Do you shag? This is a great room to shag in. My husband and I have a spacious room like this one back home which is perfect to shag in." He wondered what he'd let himself in for!

On the local *His Radio* advertising breaks, I regularly heard invitations from Seacoast, a burgeoning mega-church of 10,000+ people, to come once a month to their main campus to learn to shag ("It's a great way of making friends!"). Wow! I know churches these days are reacting to the criticisms of being out of touch and irrelevant, but is this taking things a bit too far in the name of progressive engagement with the community?!

All the above references seem shocking to an English (and to some American) ears—but not at all to South Carolinian ears. You see, the shag is the state dance. It's not achieved global fame, because (in my humble opinion) you have to look like you've just ridden a horse for way too long with the resultant piles and/or are negotiating a minefield whilst playing musical bumps. That's never going to really catch on, is it?

Communication, or rather miscommunication, will be a continuing theme of this book. As George Bernard Shaw famously said, England and the USA are two nations divided by a common language. What we say is not as important as what is heard. We think we understand what other people say, but often we get it totally wrong and only find out much later.

I had a middle-aged visitor from the States out in Burundi one time complaining, in total innocence, of her "sore fanny". To an English ear, that was way too much information! Similarly, as an Englishman in Burundi, I had to learn fast the nuances of the local language. As I studied it, my rock-star Granny (who'd worked in Africa since 1939) took great delight in explaining to me the need to understand tonal distinctions. The pronunciation of a word can completely change its meaning. For example, *gusura*, depending on how you say it, either means "to visit" or "to fart". Suffice to say, with all the different kinds of food on offer there, I've done my fair share of *visiting* over the years!

BIKE FOR BURUNDI

But back to our opening encounter. The reason I found myself at this particular church, chatting to this particular "shag instructor" on this day, was to raise awareness and ultimately sponsorship for the epic cycle ride that a few friends and I were about to embark upon. I guess we wanted to do something fairly crazy that would grab people's attention and allow us to direct them towards the plight of suffering Africans.

The team, prior to this adventure consisted of,

Geoff Morris: "Bike for Burundi" as it came to be known was all his idea. I was glad about that, since I could blame him for anything that went wrong. Geoff had already completed two trips from Land's End to John O'Groats (for the uninitiated that's from the top right tip of Britain to the bottom left, just over 1,000 miles), and so had a decent amount of experience as a cyclist. Geoff was an old mate, married to Michelle with two teenage boys, Jake and Luke. He's passionate about orphans and had spent time working in South Africa amongst the marginalized there. He's got a massive heart, a razor wit, and a big body. His training in the build-up to the ride had been significantly hampered by some unfortunate family issues, so in my mind he was the second weakest link after me. More on my physical issues below.

Craig Riley: We go back twenty years, having met each other at university (he's the same age as me). He's a Northerner and we both remember vividly our first meeting. Craig opened his mouth and spoke and I thought he was joking, putting on a funny accent, because to my untrained ear it was so broad. I started copying him ("Eee, by gum" etc.), until I noticed a change in the atmosphere which pierced even my highly underdeveloped social awareness threshold and I realized this was his normal speaking voice. I hang my head in shame thinking back to it! But we overcame that initial false start and I ended up being the best man at his wedding to Emma (where he was punching way above his weight and has moved beyond punching because they now have Beth (7) and Joel (5)). When I said I was planning to cycle across the USA, Craig didn't ask if he could join me, he just told me he was. He went so far as to sell his business and was more than ready for an adventure. Craig is physically solid and trained steadily without any injuries. I didn't anticipate he would struggle too much with making it all the way— though he is a vegetarian and I wondered whether he would starve when we reached Texas. I'd heard that in Texas they only eat vegetables made of meat.

Jeff Hennessy: I knew virtually nothing about Jeff, but I was sure we'd come to know one another intimately over the coming five weeks. He's 23 years old, and so was much younger than the rest of the cyclists, and has an explosive laugh. Jeff had heard me give a talk on Burundi at a youth event a couple of years ago and had already been planning to cycle across America himself. We just provided the perfect opportunity for him to do it. He was the most experienced cyclist and I imagined that with his age and fitness, the trip should be a relative cruise for him. He had, however, had a serious accident just eight months before, severing his Achilles tendon when falling off his bike. He had some impressively gross photos on his blog of the surgery going on inside his leg—yuck! He made a rapid recovery, but could that be a chink in his armour? We would see.

Then there was me: Simon Guillebaud. I turned 39 during the trip. Married to the gorgeous Lizzie, we have three children—Zac (6), Grace (4) and Josiah (2)—and three children are most definitely enough, thank you very much. I had the snip virtually within minutes of Josiah's birth and the German doctor became very animated when he heard my last name, which is fairly distinctive. It transpired that my Uncle John Guillebaud, amongst many other accolades, is the UK's top vasectomy man. When Herr Doktor heard we were related, his eyes bulged, his mouth salivated, and he purred, "Ah, zis is such an honour!" All that to say, I love my kids very much but we won't be having any more!

I'm the founder of Great Lakes Outreach, the charity working in Burundi that would benefit directly from our endeavour, and the common link between all these guys, who hadn't met one another until we embarked upon our journey.

THE WEAKEST LINK

So why did I consider myself to be the weakest link in the team? It dated back four months to the beginning of November. I wrote in my diary at the time,

5th November: I'd been looking forward to this three day festival of century rides for ages. I'm a cycling novice, but have been training hard for several months in preparation for my biggest physical challenge in life thus far this coming March, as four of us attempt to cycle over 3,000 miles across the USA from LA to Charleston. The distance could be likened to London to Baghdad. Could my body handle doing three days of 100 miles per day? I was feeling in good shape so thought I'd be OK. What happened?

Yesterday I launched out on my first 100 miles with about 200 other cyclists as part of Festivelo in Monck's Corner. I didn't know the route and didn't want to get lost, so I stayed towards the front, as most participants were just doing the 60-mile course. That meant I ended up, unintentionally, with the big boys, so I had to keep up with them. Actually, it was wonderfully exhilarating. I'd never been in the peloton—feeling the boost of having someone in front cut through the wind and thereby making it easier for me. I even took my turn at the head as each one peeled off. And I'll be honest with you, it felt great. Inside I was thinking: "I'm the man! This is easy. I may be the new kid on the block but I'm cruising, it's a piece of cake. I feel sorry for those slow plodders way behind us..." etc.

How wrong I was! What a moron!

I was leading the 200 cyclists. The front group was whittled down to six of us. I kept up with them for 60 miles, going way faster than I normally do. Then it was just three of us. "Yes, I really am the man!"

And then I got this progressively more searing pain in my knees. I knew I was in trouble. It very quickly dawned on me how stupid I'd been. My body just wasn't ready for what I'd put it through. I've been training at 18mph and here we were at 23mph for so long. I struggled those last few miles and went back home gloomily. I could hardly negotiate the stairs.

So this morning when I got up I was probably in denial, but I was determined to try again. Would my knees hold? Well, I knew within the first mile they wouldn't, so I quit after five miles. From leading the peloton the day before to being the first quitter on day two—from hero (not even really) to zero! What an idiot!

I'm not feeling down on myself though. I gather many others have made a similar mistake, so I'm not the first overzealous, clueless enthusiast to overdo it on his debut team run out, and I won't be the last. No, I've been laughing at myself throughout today, annoyed that I'm missing out on the challenge and camaraderie of being out there with the gang, but recognizing my pigheadedness has caused me to learn a very useful lesson before the really really big ride in March/April.

Well, I soon stopped laughing. I expected my knees to take a couple of weeks to heal, but no, four months later, despite intensive physical therapy, swimming and resting, my knees were still pathetically weak. I couldn't even lift myself off the toilet, which shows how bad things were. It was deeply discouraging. I spent some sleepless nights and was probably a grouchy git for Lizzie to have to be with. Just a few weeks before the departure date, I wrote:

17th February: Tried getting back on the bike for training after months of giving my knees a break, but no, they gave way again. And now there are only just over two weeks to go. Totally devastated...

And then the big day came to fly out to the West coast:

2nd March: I'm writing this holed up underground with a few thousand others at Cincinnati airport on my way to LA, where I've been delayed because of tornadoes which have caused twenty eight fatalities. People are very tense and it's obviously tragic for those directly affected, but only an inconvenience for me in prolonging my journey.

So as the big day for Bike for Burundi draws nearer, this is the culmination of hundreds of emails, dozens of hours of planning, thousands of miles between us of training on the road, on the treadmill, in the pool, etc. And after four months of being injured and trying to build up body strength, particularly in my knees, the moment of truth has arrived.

How do I feel? Well, I am desperate to make the whole ride. It has consumed so much of my time, focus, energy and thoughts for eight months. It's a huge dream, opportunity, challenge... And my knees are far from in a good enough state to embrace such a daunting physical experience.

I'm going to give it my best shot. I really hope they don't buckle. I need wisdom to know if I should stop. I could maybe be bloody-minded and inch forward mile by mile, but damage my knees for life—and that would be stupid and selfish, affecting not just me but also Lizzie and the kids. Or I could quit early out of fear of the former and live with the permanent regret that I didn't pull out all the stops. The human body is capable of extraordinary feats and so much of the battle is in the mind. But for me, I just want to get it right. As many people have said, it's not about the bike, there's a whole bigger picture and goal here, of raising funds and awareness for Burundi and the ongoing amazing work out there. So whatever happens to me, we are a team, and as a team we will make it, that's for sure.

So this is where I was at personally as we all met up in Los Angeles. Craig was waiting for me at the airport exit and he greeted me with the ominous news that his little boy Joel had jumped onto Daddy a little too hard a couple of days earlier and cracked his rib. He looked in real discomfort, but insisted he would be fine.

Two more people joined our team at this point, bringing our total number to six and, crucially, balancing out the nationalities so that we were now half-English and half-American. John Stinson (27) had already spent some time out in Burundi and took the role of our driver, chef and logs guru. David Strauss was on board as our videographer and documentary maker. These two had spent the last week driving an RV, on loan from a very generous guy called Todd in Charlotte, North Carolina, all the way from the East coast to LA. It was a thirty-five foot beast with a bedroom in the back and a lounge in the middle, both of which extended outwards when stationary to provide a Jacuzzi and a drinks bar. Well, not quite, but it certainly afforded some much needed floor space when all six of us were simultaneously occupying it. John gave the RV the nickname "Honey Badger" (used henceforth), essentially because it hogged the road and wouldn't back down for anyone.

So, with our team assembled and equipment in place, it was time to begin our adventure. How, I wondered, would it all play out?

CHAPTER ONE

MOUNTAIN HIGHS AND DESERT LOWS

∞ DAY 0 ∞

GEARING UP FOR THE STARTING LINE

We couldn't have had a better start—or at least a better preparation for the big start. We had been hosted by three very cool families who had looked after us superbly. California is known for its beautiful weather, beautiful beaches, beautiful people and we'd seen all of that already. Jeff's first encounter on the beach reinforced some other Californian stereotypes as a raggedy man approached him and immediately offered to share some of his marijuana. Speaking of drugs, I'm told 80-90% of the world's methamphetamines are produced in California, particularly between Sacramento and Merced.

Incidentally, in each chapter I'll be mentioning a few of the laws one can fall foul of, peculiar to each State we passed through. Here are a few things you may not know about Californian law:

Animals are banned from mating publicly within 1,500 feet of a tavern, school, or place of worship.

It is a misdemeanour to shoot at any kind of game from a moving vehicle, unless the target is a whale.

Women may not drive in a house coat.

No vehicle without a driver may exceed 60 miles per hour.

Hmm... I thought we might be guilty of jumping the odd red light, but I suspected we wouldn't struggle to remain law-abiding citizens on the whole, given the above directives.

On the Saturday during our prep we enjoyed a soirée at the house of a friend, Pastor Bob. Our team and another team from Torrance, who would be joining us on the trip, along with wives and kids, ate a lot and generally got to know one another. To complete the preparation for our own ride we watched a DVD on a big screen of what is generally reckoned to be the toughest endurance race in the world: The Race Across America (RAAM).

These guys are total nutters. The winner last year covered over 3,000 miles, passing through 12 States, on just seven and a half hours of sleep in total, spread over eight days. He was averaging nearly 400 miles per day—unbelievable!

"More people summit Everest than complete RAAM," said the women's winner. "With the Tour de France you stop at the end of the day — you rest, you get a massage, eat a meal, sleep and then start fresh the next day," she said. "But with RAAM, you don't. You're sleep-deprived and disoriented."

We are nowhere near that hardcore. We're just a bunch of Average Joes on our bikes and it's hard to compare what we're trying to do to climbing Everest or RAAM or even the Tour de France (although we're covering 850 miles more than the latter). But it's certainly our biggest lifetime challenge to date.

It was sobering to see some of the physical trials the RAAM cyclists went through, which we are sure to be confronted with as well over the next few weeks. One Englishman's neck was so weak that he could no longer hold it up, so his team strapped his head back to his shoulders so that it wouldn't just dangle down. I hope that doesn't happen to us!

∞ DAY 1 ∞
WE'RE OFF!

Finally the big day has arrived. Bring it on!

What a day it was. We were up at 5.15am to prepare to leave from just north of San Diego. We had driven the two hours down from LA to San Diego the previous night to stay at David's feisty grandmother's house so this morning would be easier. We arrived late and she was already asleep, so we only met her that morning before dawn. She's 83-years-old and told me she wasn't into cycling, but was a regular roller-blader! I was sorting out the portable ice-machine I would be carrying in order to be able to ice my knees and dropped a few ice-cubes on the floor. "Oh, leave those," she said. "Then I can slip on them and sue you!" We only had a few minutes with her before leaving, but she was obviously a real character.

Half an hour later we arrived at the beach and met up with the others from LA. There were eight extra cyclists and a team of support drivers and cooks, which would make a big difference to the first few days of the trip—a lovely start, although potentially we would be spoilt and then disappointed once they left us.

We stocked up on food, checked our tyres (US English is "tires", but English-English is what I'm going with throughout this trip since I'm English!), dipped them in the Pacific and took team photos, almost not daring to dream of hopefully all doing the same in thirty-four day's time. Would we all make it? I gave myself only a 15% chance of making it through the first day, let alone any further.

Shortly after 7.30am we kicked off up into the hills. The scenery was stunning. After a somewhat murky start to the day, the sun came out and blazed down on us. We need to average 104 miles per day on this trip and the first day's ride was mapped out at 88 miles—

deliberately a shorter day, but the lesser distance belied some additional difficulty since it was mostly uphill into the mountains for the first fifty miles. We anticipated it would be a killer.

We were twelve cyclists all together in one group at the start, but within a couple of hours and twenty-one miles Geoff had had a puncture and was strangely struggling. It seemed like the rapid onset of heat exhaustion, so we stayed together as a foursome whilst the other guys went ahead. I was grateful to the boys that they put no undue pressure on me, so we crawled along at a snail's pace and they corralled me protectively like a calf in a pod of whales, taking the brunt of any headwind and watching me from behind—I guess generally to make me feel fully supported. But I'm sure Geoff in his weakened state appreciated the pathetic pace as well.

Amazingly, the scenery got even more beautiful throughout the day, and despite the heat there was even some snow in a few places. I jumped off at one point, grabbed a handful, and managed to land a well-aimed snowball on Geoff's butt (well okay, it's not hard to miss!). Poor man, he was really struggling by the sixty mile mark with a throbbing headache and it looked like we would have to end early.

My knees, meantime, were sore and giving me some concern, but I was so excited and relieved to have made it over the hump. The last thirty miles were downhill into the desert, full of cacti and boulders; it was just awe-inspiring. We reached 46mph on the way down and Craig nearly wiped himself out by veering into a cliff wall, recovering just in the nick of time. It took a while for him to calm down afterwards as the close shave had shaken him up.

At the point of quitting, Geoff took some Ibuprofen and what must have been some illegal substances, because he promptly blasted off in front of us for the last 20 miles of the day, leaving Craig and I for dust and with the other Jeff struggling to keep up with him too.

The rest of the gang had long since arrived and we eventually hooked up at Anza-Borrego Desert State Park and enjoyed recounting our stories of the first day.

We had all made it and I was at the same time chuffed, relieved, exhausted and elated. Knowing that tomorrow we would be faced with over a hundred miles, we headed to bed early for some well-earned rest—a rest that was, at times, threatened by some horrific bowel eruptions from a certain member of the crew! It had honestly been one of the most memorable days of my life. Roll on the rest of our adventure!

∞ DAY 2 ∞
A VERY SAD, BAD, EXTRAORDINARY DAY

Nobody could have guessed how day 2 of our trip was going to pan out. It was a highly memorable day, one that stood out in the entire trip, but for all the wrong reasons. It took us a long time to get away that day. I'd been up since 4.00am. The views outside under the stars were amazing. Actually, it had taken me a while to get to sleep because of my sheer elation at having made it through the previous day. Then I had to contend with Geoff's snoring, closely followed by John's, and then Craig's—all distinct in tone, but equally effective at keeping me awake until sheer exhaustion kicked in.

We'd had breakfast with the other team and then driven off to our starting point. Geoff was still visibly exhausted, with a clanging headache, and frankly looked like death warmed up. We thought we'd have the winds with us, but actually they didn't help much in the morning. There was plenty of downhill, though, so we made good progress. The sun got hotter and hotter as we made our way. It turned out to be the hottest day of the year so far.

By the time we reached our first stop, Geoff knew he needed treatment. My Dad, who had joined our crew for the first week, rang a pharmacy and they said it sounded like Geoff had heat exhaustion and needed to stop immediately. We had a horrible conversation on the side of the road, essentially telling Geoff that he couldn't go on, because continuing would risk his life. His ride today was over. He cried and I cried too. I so understood his emotions. We'd both expected it to be me who was forced to drop out first. All those hours of training; all that money invested; the significant sacrifice of loved ones... I was devastated for him and with him. He cried out loud to God, totally broken. We did the same inside. Gutted.

Just at that moment, strangely, some Aussies drove past in a support car for a man who was running around the world! They stopped to see if they could help. The crazy man was going for a Guinness World Record. (see www.tomsnextstep.com)

We freewheeled slowly to the next town where the Honey Badger was waiting for us. Geoff got some ice on his head and went for a lie down as we followed the pharmacist's instructions. Heat exhaustion needs rest or it can lead to heat-stroke, which can easily be fatal, so we couldn't mess around with this. Geoff was desperate to carry on, despite the pain, and so he begged us to give him one hour to see if he would recover, however unlikely it seemed. We agreed, but after the hour had passed we knew he was finished. In fact, if anything, he had deteriorated.

So Craig, Jeff Junior and I got back on the bikes, knowing we had a long way to go and just a few hours to catch up with the others before sundown. I had never been so grateful for a strong tailwind as I was for the next four hours. It enabled us to blast along comfortably. As we went through the Imperial Valley, we passed Mesquite dairy farm which must have been one of the biggest in the world, with a staggering 36,000 cramped cows lying on the ground or sheltering under the myriad solar panels as far as the eye could see. One of them was shot as we whizzed by.

We were now back in amazing desert landscapes as the wind picked up some more. Visibility was vastly reduced as it gradually turned into a sandstorm. One time when we stopped for a pee, it blew right back at us and over our bikes—nice! We were in a race against time that day since I was due to speak to a youth group that evening in a place called Blythe—the last thing I felt like doing! But I didn't want to push my knees too hard. In fact, I was surprised they hadn't given in already to be honest.

What is it with me and deserts? The last time I was in one was with some mates in Wadi Rum in the Jordan fifteen years ago. We had our own truck, and at nightfall some slept in a tent, some in the truck, and Rob and I under the stars. A few hours into my deep sleep, I was rudely awakened by Rob crawling over me and running back to the truck. I pulled my head out of my sleeping bag to realise it was a raging storm. Whoosh, Rob's sleeping mat disappeared into the night. I was left splayed crab-like on the ground, desperately trying to hold down all our belongings as bits and pieces were swept irretrievably into the darkness. Meantime I overheard one of the girls in the tent exclaiming with great authority: "In Jesus' name, I command you to be still!"

On that same trip we were in Egypt, and took a road which ploughed through literally hundreds of miles of sand, with nothing as far as the eye could see other than dunes. Every 20km, there was an isolated sign informing the rare traveller how far to Cairo—280km, then 260km, then 240km, and so on. Apart from those signs, there was nothing. Rob was driving the truck, and his brother Luke was on the roof. At one stage a gust of wind blew Luke's cap off. He shouted down to Rob to turn around and fetch it. Rob reversed the truck as part of a three-point-turn, but as he did so there was a hollow clunk. He jumped out to discover he'd knocked down one of those rare signposts!

Those were some happier desert memories as we ploughed on with the sand whipping around our faces. I calculated on one stretch that I didn't need to pedal at all for five straight miles because of the tail wind. We bypassed the Chocolate Mountains, so-called because they are somehow dark brown, and ended the day with 109 miles under our belts—absolutely shattered and further weakened by the relentless sun. We made it in time, but were greeted by the news that Geoff had been admitted to hospital.

I spoke to the youth group in Blythe, having cleaned out some residual sand from my ears from the sandstorm and done a cursory wet-wipe wash to look half-decent—but I was quite sure they'd never had a filthier speaker grace their building! I also discovered this random fact: in Blythe you are not permitted to wear cowboy boots unless you already own at least two cows!

Afterwards I came out to receive yet more shocking news. Geoff's condition was serious enough to warrant him being transferred, urgently, to a heart-specialist unit some distance away. The situation had gone from bad to worse to desperate in the course of a single day and we were left waiting and wondering as doctors completed several rounds of tests. As worrying as this was, there was nothing we could do and we were forced to turn in for the night. We needed to get some sleep before the next day's pre-dawn start and another 100+ miles. We'd heard that Geoff's wonderful wife, Michelle, and his two boys were going to fly out on the next available plane. We hoped that everything would be okay and that Geoff would be sufficiently recovered to fly home to the UK as soon as possible. So sad.

We were all shell-shocked by this turn of events. Geoff was the reason we were all there in the first place. A cycling fundraiser was his idea. He'd done it for our orphanage several years ago in the UK and it was him cycling from Land's End to John o' Groats that had clinched a vital piece of land for our orphanage project in Burundi. Through the efforts of Geoff and his two companions on the trip, £40,000 had been raised. That meant we'd been able to acquire the plot of land and erect a few dormitories on it before it could be reclaimed by others in authority who might want to use it. (In Burundi, if you buy some land but don't build on it within a certain timeframe, it is basically taken off you and sold to someone else who can). I and many orphans owed a huge debt to Geoff.

Geoff is one of my favourite people on the planet. I respect him and his precious family so much. They are the kind of people who love the truth enough to live it. Words and actions go together with them. They don't just talk a good game, they live it out. Geoff was a lion of a man that day, soldiering on through unbelievable pain, and only stopping when we forced him to—a real warrior.

∞ DAY 3 ∞
LIVING TO FIGHT ANOTHER DAY!

It turned out that Geoff had had, according to initial tests, a heart attack. What?! His family members were flying out and he'd said that he wanted to see them at least one last time—although he was not optimistic about that happening. Sounds dramatic, doesn't it? But Geoff is no drama queen, I can assure you. That's how bad things looked.

But there was nothing more we could do. So as we had left to find an RV Park on the Colorado River to get some much-needed sleep, a couple of hours later Geoff was being flown out, after the sandstorm had subsided. On the evacuation paperwork there was a box to be filled in entitled "Disease-specific risk" and the medics had simply written "death". That said it all. My Dad was a legend in helping speed up the proceedings at the local hospital and looked after Geoff all the while he was in the E.R., but they wouldn't let Dad go in the helicopter as Geoff was moved to the heart unit. Without batting an eyelid David, our videographer, offered to drive Dad the two hours to Palm Springs' specialist cardio unit, knowing he would not get back until 4.00am. Wow, every member of our team was playing their part!

Meanwhile, I slept terribly. I was awake from 2.00am with a headache and thinking about Geoff, Michelle and their boys, Jake and Luke. My headache might have been caused by dehydration, despite the fact that I'd drunk 14 bottles of water and/or Gatorade the day before. So I drank two more, which meant countless trips to the tiny toilet until dawn.

There was a sombre mood in our camp as we thought about Geoff and hoped he was going to be okay. I forced myself to eat the equivalent of three breakfasts in one, because it's so hard to take on the required 6,000 calories per day you need to fuel the body. It meant that I felt like vomiting for the next hour or so.

We set off at 7.30am. When you're aiming for 100 miles in a day, starting off at a speed of just 6mph because of a nasty headwind is very discouraging. It meant very slow progress through to lunchtime. At one point I was deep in thought, plodding along, with the other two behind me discussing directions, when suddenly two massive, fierce mongrels appeared from nowhere and ambushed us in a cunning pincer movement. They both started on me, and I was able to kick one in the mouth as he tried to bite me. He beat a hasty retreat after that and the other dog moved away to attack Jeff. In retrospect, it was a funny spectacle, but in the heat of the moment quite traumatising and it took a while for the adrenaline rush to subside!

In time we crossed over the Colorado River from California into Arizona—the second of ten states we would ride through on our journey. We were now in real cactus country. Speaking of which, apparently there is a possible twenty-five year prison sentence meted out to anyone caught cutting one down. Craig, slightly idiotically, pressed his finger onto a prickle to see if it really was as sharp as they are reputed to be. He then seemed surprised and even aggrieved that it drew blood! Further Arizona idiosyncrasies include the following:

It is unlawful to refuse a person a glass of water (makes sense).

Hunting camels is prohibited (not seen any of those).

Any misdemeanour committed while wearing a red mask is considered a felony (are they colour-prejudiced?)

Donkeys cannot sleep in bathtubs (either they specialise in big bathtubs or small donkeys).

It is illegal to manufacture imitation cocaine (but okay if it's the real thing?)

When being attacked by a criminal or burglar, you may only protect yourself with the same weapon that the other person possesses (lots of potential Monty Pythonesque sketches could come out of that).

Cycling-wise, day 3 felt distinctly discouraging. Because of the strong head wind we covered only 82 miles. But my knees were also to blame, holding me back and slowing all of us down. Craig and Jeff, who are both fit and strong, could have done a century without much trouble, but they patiently allowed me to dictate the pace. They don't put any pressure on me at all, which is a real relief. It's difficult for me because I know that if I push it, my knees will give way and my cycling will be over. But at the same time, we simply don't have much time to play with, so we need to push forward.

Just minutes before we were due to call it a day I had a puncture, which was probably the best timing possible. We packed up and drove a fair way to a house that had been made available to us for the night. Then we received the best news imaginable in an email from Dad: Geoff was in the clear! What a relief! We gave a corporate cry of delight. It meant that, panic over, Geoff would be able to re-join us in a few days and slowly build up the miles again—a wonderful morale booster after a discouraging day. Tomorrow would be another long one, but I had already made it further than I thought I would. So all of us (including and especially Geoff) would live to fight another day!

∞ DAY 4 ∞

SURPRISE CONFESSIONS OF A HOLY MAN WITH A DODGY GUT

The day got off to an ignominious start for me. For the second night in a row I awoke at 2.00am utterly dehydrated and never returned to sleep. I drank three bottles of water and ate two bananas whilst lying on my bed thinking about how daunting this attempt is. A large part of the challenge is that there is so little room for anything to go wrong. Losing time at any point would be a real blow and on day 4, something did go wrong.

I've already spoken about sleep; then there is food. It is incredibly hard to eat enough during the day to take on board the required calories. And cramming the food on board literally plays havoc with your gut. Jeff and I alternated in running to the toilet to do our *thang*. Jeff, gentleman that he is, actually interrupted his own "evacuations" at one point in order to let me in, desperate as I was (one of the benefits of being the leader!). To compound things, I was suffering from stomach cramps.

I woke everyone up at 5.00am so we could drive to our starting point, which that day was quite a long way away. Two days on and we were still picking grains of sand out of our ears from that crazy sandstorm. It had been a bitterly cold night and when we set off it was still very cold—but actually it's much nicer to cycle in those cold hours after being exposed to so much sun.

The road we took was pretty much straight for 50 miles—so actually very dull, in fact—but we made good time and stopped for lunch after 55 miles. On the way we came across a bearded, scruffy-looking guy who'd been walking across the USA for the last five months. Good effort!

We passed through Wickenburg en route, the best known of the old gold camp cities lying on the Hassayampa River and forming part of the Golden Triangle. It's named after Henry Wickenburg who threw a rock at a stubborn mule in 1863 (so the story goes) and the rock was heavy with gold, so it fell far short. That's where fortuitous Henry started digging. It's still a popular haunt for amateur gold prospectors who, at the end of the process of sifting, will shout out the age-old cry, "Colour in my pan!" if they've got lucky.

Craig's front derailleur started causing problems and needed fixing. By some beautiful coincidence the mechanic who worked at the only bike shop in town was taking a day off, but happened to drop in for something just as Craig arrived. Excellent!

Later that afternoon, when we stopped briefly at a Shell station, Jeff discovered that two of his spokes had broken off and one of his wheels was bent. We'd made such good time up until then that this was potentially a total spanner in the works. The day's ride looked set to finish there at 2.30pm, costing us 50 miles, but no, John, our driver, arrived right on cue (normally we would only hook up after a few hours) and he had Geoff's bike on board. However, the cleats didn't match Jeff's (for non-cyclists, you clip your shoe into the pedals and there tend to be four main designs. In this case they didn't match—aargh!).

But let me rewind a bit. Last Saturday, when we were still in LA preparing for the trip, Geoff and Jeff were walking down the street with their host family and came to a friend's yard sale. They chatted about *Bike for Burundi,* and the husband, Bob McManus, promptly offered his high-quality Felt racer as a donation. Wow! That just seemed too generous, so they turned down the offer. But when Geoff told me about it later, I decided we should go back and take him up on the offer. His wife couldn't believe he was giving it away and there seemed to be a little tension in the air all of a sudden, but he insisted and we took off with it before he had time to change his mind. Well, Bob, you total legend! Lo and behold, Jeff's cleats matched his pedals! We could continue on our way. The bike obviously hadn't been used in months as the chain was filthy, but after some cleaning work, we were good to go again.

This time we blasted off with a decent tailwind under the baking sun. We came to the encouragingly-named town of Surprise, just outside Phoenix. There had been some other fun town names along the way (Organ Pipe, Tombstone, Santa Claus, Why?, Hog Eye, Monkey's Eyebrow—yes, these are all bona fide Arizona town names!). In fact, the previous day when I had been discouraged by our lack of progress, head down and plodding on, the others had called out to me to look up. We were entering the small town of Hope! Just that small sign was a real boost to me. Then a few hundred yards later as we exited the hamlet, there was another sign which read "Beyond Hope"!

But back to Surprise. The confession referred to at the beginning of this section is mine. Can I really stoop so low as to share it with you? Aargh, okay. My gut, as already mentioned, had been playing up as we adapted to eating weird foods in silly quantities. So as we cycled along one busy street, I shifted in my seat, released a cheeky trouser cough (as I've taught my kids to call them) and promptly followed through—a veritable shitastrophe! I couldn't believe it had happened; I can't believe I'm now broadcasting the fact to the world in print either! But actually, it's important to let you know how big a deal the physiological dimension of such a challenge is—so I'm giving you the real picture in the name of transparency, as unedited as I dare!

Conveniently (looking for a silver lining to this cloud!), this happened just as we passed a garage. I delicately got off my bike and asked a friendly Mexican mechanic if I could use his bathroom, where I hastily disappeared to restore some personal dignity. There you go, that's the (Surprise) confession of a (supposed) holy man with impressive gut rot! Enough said.

Wonderfully, in the meantime, John was able to have Jeff's bike fixed. We got a bit lost because of road works and eventually stopped as dusk fell. But the great news was that we had managed to cover 115 miles—15 more than was planned for the day. Amazing, considering how it could have been sabotaged due to both Craig and Jeff's bike issues. However, things were about to get a bit tougher…

CHAPTER TWO

NO PAIN, NO GAIN

∞ DAY 5 ∞

THE TOUGHEST DAY YET

It was a humdinger of a day. In fact, it made the first day's ride up into the mountains from the beach outside San Diego look like a stroll in the park. It was also my luscious Lizzie's birthday, so I was sad not to be with her to celebrate together. What a great woman and what a lucky man I am!

We always knew this was going to be difficult, so could we possibly make it with the state of my knees slowing us down? Probably not, but we'd try.

Backtracking to the previous night, we had been hosted by David and Corry Wells—relatives of a friend of mine in Mt Pleasant—and they were just superb. We were fed royally, they washed our dirty linen, and bent over backwards to do whatever we asked. I have seldom been so tired in my life, but I still took a pill to help me sleep beyond 2.00am, as had been my norm thus far. It worked and that sleep was much needed. A 5.30am breakfast enabled us to get away by 6.15am, but it was a fair drive to the starting point.

It took us 38 miles under the fierce sun to get out of the sprawl of Phoenix/Tempe—the urban sprawl just seemed to go on and on. At

one stage we cycled past the Chicago Cubs doing their spring training. Dad then left us and flew back to Charleston to be with Lizzie
and the family. It was great to have him with us for the first few days
and he totally came into his own when Geoff needed someone to
kick butt on his behalf at the ER, and then with the medical evacuation by helicopter, keeping Geoff company until his family arrived.
I'm proud of my Dad! Geoff was on the mend, albeit slowly, and
enjoying some time with his family in Palm Springs, where he
needed to rest for at least the next 11 days.

We passed the Superstition Mountains, which apparently contain
a lot of gold, although only one man in history seems to have been
able to find any consistently. Way back in the 1870s, a German
called Jacob Walz returned from his explorations with several
mule-loads of rich ore. He would disappear from time to time
(despite many people keeping a close eye on him in order to glean
his secrets) only to reappear several months later with loads more
of the stuff. On his deathbed in 1891 he left a riddle which has
perplexed and frustrated generations of gold-seekers. If you can
solve it, that Caribbean Island can be yours, not to mention the
cruise!

"There's a stone face looking up at my mine. If you pass three red
hills, you've gone too far. The rays of the setting sun shine on my
gold. Climb above my mine and you can see Weaver's Needle."

We soon came to the mother of all climbs into some more mountains: 4 miles at a 6° incline. As if that wasn't enough, there was also
a headwind. To compound things further, my derrière was incredibly
sore. Because of my knees being injured for the last several months,
I have barely sat in the saddle (unlike the others, who therefore have
more "acclimatised" backsides) and today's ride brings our tally of
hours riding to 40 in the last 5 days. It really is a pain in the butt! So
I sit down for as long as I can bear and then I stand and pedal upright

for a few moments' relief, which uses up lots more energy and so can't be sustained.

Sometimes with the incline and the wind, we were down to 5mph, which makes for a long day and very slow progress. It really was a question of miles, not smiles, as the miles almost begrudgingly accumulated. We came across a delightful English threesome (parents and their son from Devon) who were riding the same route as us, but with no support vehicle i.e. carrying their tent, food, clothing etc., in panniers on their bikes - in other words, much more hardcore than us, although they were taking a few more days to do it. They joined us in the Honey Badger for a quick chat, drink and food, before we ploughed on.

And on and on and on we went. At the pinnacle of the mountain, 24,000 feet up (well, not quite, but it felt like that), there was a store called "Top of the World Hardware" or some such name. It did feel like we were at the top of the world: an amazing view of some gorgeous scenery. But frankly we were too exhausted to really appreciate it.

Opposite the hardware store was a hairdressing salon called "Curl Up 'n' Dye", followed by "I. Gassum & E. Pullsem, No-Nonsense Dentistry". Above them were a couple of legal practices called "Ditcher, Quick and Hyde Divorce Lawyers", and "Swindle and Cheetham". Around the corner was a garish sigh: "Stitchem and Leggit—Used Car Dealers", and then a liquor store called "Ales of the Unexpected". Well, both body and mind were breaking down a little by this point so maybe some of the latter were figments of my imagination, who knows. We have way too much time spent in our own heads on this trip!

Daylight was fading and we faced a race against the clock to make it down the other side, even though we were wiped out. The temperature dropped starkly as we left and now instead of thinking of our sun-burnt faces, our teeth were chattering in the cold.

We made it all the way to the next city, Globe, Arizona, and promptly collapsed on the floor of the Honey Badger in exhausted elation. A quirky local law states that in Globe, cards may not be played in the street with a Native American. Not sure what that's all about. Today's coverage was "only" 95 miles, but wow, did we work for them. It was easily the hardest day's ride so far and I hoped my knees would recover for the next day, because they were calling out progressively louder for me to stop. Actually, both Craig and I are walking gingerly, like bandy-legged old men, ascending and descending any steps we encounter sideways. Some kind person had donated us rooms at a local hotel, so we had a place to crash, have a shower, get scrubbed up, and chomp a few thousand more calories before falling into bed.

∞ DAY 6 ∞
PAINFUL PROGRESS

We were on the road by 7.00am and made good progress at first. We were at high altitude, so were wrapped up in all our cold gear. In fact, we saw clouds for the first time this week, which was a pleasant change. Soon enough, we had our second dog encounter. As with the previous attack, I just had my head down looking at the road and would have got the shock of my life had Jeff not shouted from behind me.

I looked up to see three big black bitches bearing down on us, fangs specially sharpened for the occasion. I jumped off my bike and shouted at Craig to do the same. As soon as you're off your bike, most of these frothing monsters instantly turn into docile softies. But Craig insisted on continuing to cycle, so Jeff and I were treated to a few hundred yards of hilarity with him trying to shoo them away, shouting "Nooooo! Noooo!" as they snarled at his rotating legs! We laughed our heads off. In fact, I chuckled repeatedly throughout the day as I relived the experience and am now as I write about it.

At one stage we came across a biker gang. We were in the middle of nowhere (the scene of much of our adventure), but there was a shabby journeyman's café. About forty guys, hairy, leather-clad and mean-looking, were standing around their eclectic selection of bikes. So far on this trip I had greeted any onlookers with great gusto as we passed by, but this time I kept my eyes focused dead ahead, imagining what they must be thinking of the three, strange-looking men clad in Lycra leotards, attempting to pass by inconspicuously. Sure enough, to reinforce my prejudices, a couple of miles later, I was cycling marginally on the main road (as opposed to the cycle lane—the reason for doing so will be explained below), when the bikers blasted past and ran me off the road.

Why was I not completely in the cycling lane? Because I was in so much pain. The cycle lanes have more bumps in them. From the first hour, the deep bruising in my backside meant that I had a routine of sitting in the saddle for 3 minutes and then standing to cycle for 1 minute. Back in 1996 I had hitchhiked from Kigali, Rwanda to Arusha, Tanzania. It was only a few hundred miles and I thought it would take me just over a day. Well, it took three full days and was the worst journey of my life.

One stretch of travel involved two kids sitting on my completely numb lap for six hours and one of them vomiting all over me. Another stretch involved being sat in the back of a cramped "combi" for 3 hours (seating capacity of 16) with 26 other sweaty people and, from the get-go, looking down at my seat and discovering it didn't exist. Where a seat had once been located, now there was only a vertical, tubular metal rod. I held myself hovering over this rod for the entire 3 hour journey hoping I wouldn't be impaled! I can safely say that Day 6's ride was the most painful day for my backside since that horrible experience! I winced and grimaced aplenty as we ground out the miles.

We arrived in a place called Safford and stopped at the traffic lights. There was a biker in the lane next to me straddling a beautiful three-wheel machine with a stars-and-stripes bandana on his head. He said nonchalantly, "Are you guys with Bike for Burundi?" I was astounded, wondering how he could possibly have heard of us.

"Yes!" I replied. "How did you know?"

"Do I look like a pastor to you?" he replied enigmatically. Then the lights changed and he roared off, leaving us somewhat bemused.

We discovered later that he was indeed a pastor (a refreshingly unconventional-looking one!) called Dr Phil, and some of our team would be visiting his church the following day. But in the meantime, we still had 35 miles to cover. We'd clocked up 77 miles before a late lunch and had been too long on the road without a good meal due to some miscommunication between us and the Honey Badger. We realised we couldn't let that happen again, because it was too easy to wipe out through lack of food and water.

Craig was really struggling with diarrhoea. Hey, we were all struggling with our guts because of having to eat so much, but that day it had hit Craig hard. He had been battling to eat enough food— it was just plain difficult to swallow enough fuel during the course of a day. So the last stretch was a bit of a grind.

We came across a man pushing a shopping cart miles from any-where and so stopped off to say a quick hi. His name was Bryan. His Dad had died and he was on his way to Austin. He'd been walking for two months. Wow! Taking on an endeavour like this, you're bound to meet some extraordinary people along the way. But being pushed for time meant we missed out on personal encounters. That frustrated me. I rode back down the hill, recognising that this guy was hurting, and asked if I could pray for him. He was keen, so I did. I just prayed that he would meet God on his crazy journey through such beautiful scenery. He was grateful. Bryan, if you're reading this, I hope you found the Way on your personal spiritual journey.

That meeting so energized me that I was able to blast up the mountain to catch up with the others. Then we sailed down the other side as the sun was setting and the temperature was dropping sharply. It was then a race against time to travel back to Safford in the Honey Badger to enjoy a lovely meal with our hosts. We all split up to stay with different families and were looking forward to a day off the next day.

We'd covered 109 miles and the feeling of exhaustion and satisfaction were indescribable. Here ended the first week—well, almost. Tomorrow we would do a gentle "recovery" ride of a few miles, since we reckoned that the coming Monday would be the hardest of all 34 days.

∞ DAY 7 ∞
TRASHED

We arrived back in Safford trashed. The great folks at First Baptist were waiting for us with a gorgeous meal, which we scoffed down, before we split up to stay at four different hosts for the night. I was with the Smiths, a delightful family with two little boys. I really needed my sleep, but in between at least a dozen or so trips to the bathroom during the night to deal with my gut issues, I got maybe two hours. During my fleeting bouts of half-sleep I think I was paranoid about "leaving my mark" in a highly memorable but inappropriate way on the bed of kind 11-year-old Andrew, who had vacated it for me for a couple of nights. "Oh yeah, I remember that missionary guy with diarrhoea who…"—you get my drift!

Sleep is crucial and I'm just not getting it, so it was interesting when I Skyped my sister Rebecca in England. I think she was in a pub watching the England v France rugby match and, as we talked, I just burst into tears. I'm not sure she even noticed, since the line was a bit fuzzy. But talking to someone I loved unexpectedly triggered a switch and opened the floodgates, allowing all of the tension and exhaustion that I had been trying to ignore to come flooding out. Afterwards I looked through a few pictures of Lizzie and the kids and the tears flowed again. I've watched documentaries of tough men (far tougher than me, I'm not for a moment putting myself in that category) doing incredible feats of endurance and slowly being broken down. I guess that's what happened—not just to me, but to all of us.

Shortly afterwards I received a message on Facebook from my best Burundian buddy, John:

Dear Simon and friends,

We cannot thank you enough for what you're doing for us. We keep reading your blogs and all of us are praying for you, including the orphans in Homes of Hope. Yes, we understand the pains you're going through, which are maybe a small taste of the kind of suffer-ings that the nine million Burundians have been going through since 1993. Thank God that for you, it's just physical and only for 34 days! Here in Burundi most people have no hope for the future.

There was an attack at Gihanga on Thursday this week and three policemen died. Teachers who are 83% of the governmental workers are on strike. Civil society has called all the organizations to join teachers for a bigger strike this week, because life is so grim here now—worse than you saw last year, because even the few people who have jobs can no longer feed their kids any more. All prices keep going higher and higher, almost on a weekly basis, while there is no money in the country. People are starving.

Thanks a million, once again, dear brothers for the pains you all are going through in order to help us in our sufferings here in the heart of Africa.

It reminded me why we were doing what we were doing—and it was good to put things in perspective.

The next morning I spoke twice at First Baptist in their morning services. Due to sheer exhaustion I repeatedly felt on the edge of tears. But it went well and the people seemed genuinely impacted and challenged.

This day was a recovery day—not a rest day, but a recovery one. We had a brief ride planned to keep the muscles and miles ticking over, knowing that Monday and Tuesday were going to be nasty as we headed up and down some more mountains. We got 17 miles done, a lot of it very steep up into the mountains, and it felt good to get that under our belts. The beauty of the rugged scenery was literally awe-inspiring.

We returned in time for me to speak at the evening meeting, standing on leaden legs, and again it was a fruitful opportunity. It was such fun to meet new people along our trip who were so supportive and generous. Our taste of Safford had been a sweet one, thanks to biking pastor Ken and his gang!

Looking back over our week, Monday through Saturday, we had completed 88 miles, then 109, 82, 115, 95 and finally 109. The first two weeks were meant to be the hardest and at this point we were half way through them, before embarking on three "easier" weeks that led to the finish in Charleston, South Carolina.

In terms of the three of us, I still felt like the weakest link due to my knees and my chaffing backside (I managed to get some Sudocrem to treat myself, which is basically used to treat babies with butt rash!). But I thought that if I could get through the coming week then I might be quietly confident of making it to the end. You'll recall that at the start I'd given myself just a 15% chance of getting through day 1.

I was the slowest because of my knee injuries but, paradoxically, I was able to go up the mountains fastest. It strained them too much for me to stay in the saddle, so I did most of it standing, which drained more energy but gave me more speed. Craig probably had the strongest legs, and had a great kick to him when he wanted to suddenly take off, but he struggled the most with taking on enough food, and so was frequently the most trashed at the end of the day. Jeff was always going to be the strong link because he's fifteen years younger than us and was already a keen and experienced cyclist. But he still got some aches due to his previous Achilles tendon injury.

∞ DAY 8 ∞
PUNCTURE PROS IN NEW MEXICO

After taking another sleeping pill the previous evening in order to get a reasonable night's rest, we rendezvoused at 5.30am from our four different locations and set off for the start of the ride. 8-year-old Grant, my little host for the weekend, had left me an envelope on the table with some kind words, a lovely picture, and $2.25 to contribute towards our fundraising, which was really touching. It was freezing cold to begin with as we were high up in the mountains and before long we had left Arizona and entered New Mexico. The roads in New Mexico were not terrible by any stretch, but definitely worse than Arizona, so Craig ended up having four punctures and Jeff one, which knocked about an hour off our day.

NO PAIN, NO GAIN

After one puncture repair, we'd barely gone a hundred yards when my bike slid in the gravel and I came off it. I was fine, but Craig was right behind and bumped into me. Then, with his feet still stuck in the cleats, he fell sideways along with his bike down the embankment. It seemed minor enough, and it always looks comical when someone falls sideways to the floor helplessly still clicked in by their feet, but actually it was quite serious because he further damaged his cracked rib. He found the whole day, therefore, much more challenging, along with his bad gut and sore eyes. Adding to this his inability to take on board enough food meant that he "bonked" (a technical term meaning to lose all energy. The original title to this book was going to be "Bonking on a Bike for Burundi, but my folks said they'd disown me if I went ahead with it!) before the end of the day. To his credit, despite being drained of all energy, he ground out the last 14 miles and we ended up with 98 miles on the clock—more than we set out to do because of the climbs.

I found it quite an easy day and would have liked to get more miles done, but I guess the other two have felt the same on several occasions about me with my weak knees, and yet exhibited great patience. That's what teamwork is all about. My backside is a whole lot better. Yesterday Ken gave me his gel seat to put on top of my razor blade one and that helped. There was still some chafing going on, because most of the bits of clothing I'm wearing are old hand-me-downs, so we stopped off and bought some stuff at a bike shop in Silver City, bumping into the same English family threesome from a few days ago. There was also an English lad working on the bikes who was listening to the Premier League and bemoaning Arsenal just scoring a winner against Newcastle five minutes into stoppage time, so that was an added bonus as I'm a Gooner!

The one funny event of the day was when we crested a hill and came across a completely new type of parched terrain. Craig said, "If it was green, it would be really lush around here." To which Jeff, who is colour blind, agreed, "Yes, it's so green and lush here!"

That night we slept in the Honey Badger in an RV park. Tomorrow we faced the biggest climb of all for the remainder of our trip.

∞ DAY 9 ∞
TOO MUCH SEWAGE AND SUN TO BE FUN!

The day didn't get off to a good start. If you haven't seen the film "RV" starring Robin Williams, I give it a strong recommendation. In it he has a very messy sewage accident on what is a nightmare family vacation. Our Honey Badger's water and sewage system hasn't been working for a while. John drove it over to have the tank of sewage emptied, and the connecting tube which was cracked actually broke away, spewing out our previous week's refuse and emitting, as you'd expect, some fairly choice smells. The cheerful operator in charge of the sewage was way too laid back about it—like it happened all the time.

That changed our day's plans because John would have to drive all the way to Las Cruces (our end destination 113 miles away) to get it fixed. This in turn meant that David, our video man, would need to be our shadow that day—on hand to replenish our liquids and foods, and to take our excess clothing from us once the initial freezing temperatures had dissipated.

The actual ride began beautifully. On the way up the mountain, I saw a few deer effortlessly bounding over 5ft fences with such grace-fulness, it was an uplifting sight. There was plenty of snow about. Craig came across some big animal footprints and we were on the lookout for bears, but none came into view. At one stage I jumped off my bike to throw a snowball at the others. It's so weird to have snow when the sun is out and it gets really hot during the day. Craig won the competition for writing his name most clearly in the snow with his pee—it looked like a cross between Times New Roman and Arial (sorry ladies, but boys will be boys! Of course, it wasn't my idea to have this competition; but I reluctantly took part because of intense peer pressure, despite being low on ammunition at the time).

We had concerns that Craig's cracked rib would make the mountain climb go too slowly, but actually we made good time to the top and reached Emory Pass, where we were greeted with another awe-inspiring view. Then it was 30 miles downhill at top speed, having to watch out for black ice in the mountain shadows.

I didn't think it was going to be hard post Emory Pass, but actually it was a looooong day. The sun was belting down on us, the wind didn't go in our favour until near the end, and because we didn't have the Honey Badger, we didn't get a decent lunch. Those three factors combined to knock the stuffing out of us. It dragged on and on and I pushed my knees too hard, which was gutting because I thought they had strengthened sufficiently. For the last 40 miles in the desert I had shooting pains up my legs, warning me to stop quickly. But we had to make it to the end. Then a headache kicked in. Jeff was totally shattered too and Craig looked progressively more like a zombie with his cracked lips, chafing nether regions from forgetting his afternoon dose of chamois cream, and eyes pouring from the melted sun cream coming down from his forehead. He could hardly even see where he was going, poor chap, but he was a brick, totally rock solid!

We got chased by five different dogs, three alone in the hamlet of Garfield. The word "Garfield" used to conjure up for me images of the lazy, genteel cat. Now it elicits a picture of snarling canines drooling in anticipation of a kill. There were lots of dead animals along our way—one massive Doberman corpse, stiff with rigor mortis, two skunks, a snake, and a cat.

Some days are fun. Today wasn't one of them. The thought of that relentless sun bearing down on us day after day was daunting. I never thought I'd prefer to cycle in the rain, but today it would have made a nice change. We stumbled into the Honey Badger as the sun disappeared below the horizon and lay on the floor, as tired as we'd ever been. I felt dehydrated, confused and trance-like, with a head-ache to boot. David videoed a quick interview with me, which would go down as being one of my less coherent ones, but we wanted to capture the reality of the challenge on film. It showed the true extent of our pathetic condition!

That night we booked into a Hampton Inn at a special discount. A very kind friend of a friend of Dad's who lectures at the nearby uni-versity took us all out for an Italian meal. I mistakenly ordered two main meals and couldn't eat much of either as I'd already pigged out on the free bread. But maybe it was a fortuitous mistake because at least I'd be able to have them tomorrow for lunch whilst the others enjoyed less sophisticated fare.

CHAPTER THREE

DESOLATE MIND GAMES

∞   DAY 10   ∞

SQUISHED SKUNKS AND BORDER CONTROL

Disclaimer: Something in this chapter isn't true—I'm just trying to keep you on your toes, but I wonder if you'll be able to work out which bit? Day 10 began with some dread on my part after the previous day's hard slog in the sun, although thankfully my splitting headache had cleared. But in fact it turned out to be our easiest day so far, finishing early at 5.00pm after completing 110 miles because we had a long drive back to El Paso for an evening engagement.

We'd got off to an early start to maximize the coolness, so were on the road shortly after sunrise. Las Cruces, by the way, is a university town, population 80,000, and second biggest city in New Mexico after Albuquerque. New Mexico is the second poorest state after Mississippi. We were told last night that there is a big drink-driving problem here (every once in a while we came across flowers and a crucifix on the roadside where someone had died, frequently with a sign above it warning of the dangers), and lots of restaurants have signs outside saying "No Guns Allowed Inside". The one law I discovered that was peculiar to Las Cruces states that "you may not carry a lunchbox down Main Street". There must be some historical incident behind it, but I couldn't find out what it was.

The road was kind to us, gently sloping with a nice tailwind as well, so my knees were able to take it easier. It was one of those ghastly dogs yesterday that made me push hard on the pedals to avoid a munching that strained and reversed the progress I thought they'd made—very annoying. We drove past a town called "Truth or Consequences" (check it out on Google), named after a game-show in the 1950s that agreed to give the town advertising on the show if they agreed to the name—hmm…

We were very near the Mexican border and so there were lots of Border Control police trucks speeding past at various intervals to prevent illegal immigrants entering from across the way. There was an uncanny number of squished skunks—I counted five within a few miles—and they're obviously not the most talented animals at crossing roads, but they have been bred by the US Border Agency as a deterrent to Mexicans on this stretch as they often emit their pungent odours when detecting fear. Apparently, they are extremely sensitive to fear in humans who are seeking to evade the authorities (check this out on Google also!). Well, they certainly smell once they've been dead a few days, I can vouch for that.

And then it was goodbye New Mexico and hello Texas. We were now into our fourth state, so vast it should be a country in itself. There were loads of pecan trees which made me reminisce about a time I was visiting Nacogdoches, Texas, about a decade ago. I was being initiated into the breakfast pancake scene and a lady said to me: "Do you want budder'pkahn on that?" I asked what on earth budder'pkahn was. "You're telling me you don't know what budder'pkahn is?" she asked incredulously. Those around the table were equally staggered at my sheltered upbringing. Eventually we established it was butter pecan with at least four syllables in it—a good memory for a private chuckle as row upon row of pecan trees passed me by. That same lady was the one who asked me in all seriousness: "Wow, so you speak four languages—English, French, German and African?"

Actually, a friend, Ron Banks (who is joining us for the last week of our trip through Alabama, Florida and South Carolina) and I had a similar conversation on a hike in the mountains of North Carolina. He shared some trail mix with me and I said, "Hmm, nice, has that got (phonetically) 'bnahhna' in it?" He didn't get me: "What did you say?" "Has that got 'bnahhna' in it?" "Say what?" "You know, 'bnahhna'. "I don't understand." Then I said it the American way: "Ba-NANA!" How we laughed! Yes, we English and Americans are two nations divided by a common language. And this trip was always fun on that level because of our diverse backgrounds.

Since we will be spending the next few pages in Texas, let me share a few of the quirky laws we were sure to respect and endorse:

It is illegal to take more than three sips of beer at a time while standing.

A recently passed anti-crime law requires criminals to give their victims 24-hours notice, either orally or in writing, and to explain the nature of the crime to be committed.

The entire Encyclopaedia Britannica is banned in Texas because it contains a formula for making beer at home.

When two trains meet each other at a railroad crossing, each shall come to a full stop, and neither shall proceed until the other has gone.

It is illegal to drive without windshield wipers. You don't need a windshield, but you must have the wipers.

You can be legally married by publically introducing a person as your husband or wife three times.

It is illegal to shoot a buffalo from the second story of a hotel.

It is illegal to milk another person's cow.

Back to the ride: we made such quick progress (it's all relative) that it did a world of good for our morale. David headed off to the airport to fly back home for 10 days to earn some money for a change, rather than just serving us here *pro bono*. He'd been a massive asset and bailed us out a couple of times when we would have been stuffed otherwise (as in the time Geoff had to go to hospital, and up in the mountains when the Honey Badger needed fixing because of the broken sewage pipe).

Almost all of my cycling gear was old clothing donated by cycling buddies and one of the tops has "US Army" emblazoned across it. I was wearing it as we went through the Border Control roadblock and whilst others were being stopped and questioned, the official waved us through. Was it because of the top? Well, if so, good job he didn't get to hear my atrocious attempts at a US accent, which may start reasonably in Southern drawl for a few words, but quickly morphs into a bastardized Punjabi/Welsh twang!

At the end of the day it was back onto the Honey Badger to be buffeted around as we headed back into El Paso (75% of the population here speak Spanish). Craig was sat in the back with me but eventually had to move, since John was enjoying the bouncy roads a bit too much and Craig hit the lowered cupboard ceiling above us and bashed his head. We couldn't be too cross with John, however—he's a hilarious bloke, a great team player, and that day was his 26th birthday. So another day, another mini-victory. As the Burundi proverb says: "Buhoro buhoro, ni rwo rugendo." Slowly, slowly, we'll get there.

∞   DAY 11   ∞
BALL-SPLITTING WAR STORIES ON THE ROAD IN TEXAS

The previous night I ended up speaking at two meetings. We were hosted by this superb lady, Kelly, who had been at the Citadel (a military school like Sandhurst or West Point) with both John (our driver) and Olivia (who is GLO National Director in Burundi right now, filling my shoes). In fact, Olivia had had a massive influence on Kelly's life at the Citadel and now Kelly was a similarly impressive lady, recently back from a tour of duty in Afghanistan; passionate, focused, generous, a go-getter, etc. She had fixed us up to speak to these two groups and some food was lined up. She'd even gone the extra mile in baking us home-made energy bars and sending us off with breakfast at 5.15am. What more could you ask for?

El Paso's history is interesting. It is set in a low pass at the point where Texas meets Mexico and New Mexico. It was too isolated to be much affected by the Texas revolution, but the gold rush of 1849 meant much more traffic, including railroads and a military post that became Fort Bliss. The famous, fickle Rio Grande ("a mile wide and a foot deep, too thin to plough and too thick to drink") often shifted its course, which led to constant territorial disputes. One such shift led to significant gains for Texas, which eventually went to arbitration in 1911.

Although Mexico was awarded the disputed land, the US refused to accept the ruling. Meantime in 1917, a huge underground lake was discovered which meant that despite being a rain-starved desert, lush irrigated fields were now possible, rendering the whole area much more sustainable. It was only in 1963 that a review board awarded Mexico 436 acres and Texas 193, which meant that several thousand Americans needed to be relocated to US soil. Presidents Lyndon B. Johnson and Gustavo Diaz Ortaz met and agreed to endorse the new settlement.

We had a 60 mile drive back to the start of our route, because we were making such good progress and were ahead of our planned pace. The wind had been with us, but at the beginning of the day my knees were really dodgy, so we'd begun slowly and horrible thoughts were creeping back into my mind that I might not be able to make it. At one stage in the corner of my eye I saw a ball of fur moving behind the brush parallel to us and presumed it was another dog on our tails. But if it was, it would have to be a lardy one because it was almost as round as it was high. Then it burst through the undergrowth and shocked us in our tracks because it was a wild boar/warthog-type creature.

A lot of Day 11 was spent on Interstate-10 (the equivalent of a motorway in England and just a few States allow cyclists on them here). We crossed from Mountain to Central Time Zone. A week ago we were in Pacific, then Arizona (one of only two States that never changes time), and in the mix there was a daylight saving time change with clocks going forward, so we were all a bit confused. We'd experienced four time changes as we'd covered these last several hundred miles by bike.

The sun was out, but not as brutal as other days, and we enjoyed clouds in the sky providing further protection. When Jeff was rubbing sun-cream into his face and ears at one point, I remarked, "Wow, you really have quite decent-sized ears, don't you?" John guffawed: "I love the way you Brits disguise your insults in such polite language!" I was actually genuinely admiring his impressive pair! Then, as we cycled along (you have to understand, we have hours to kill, sometimes in silent reverie, sometimes talking banalities, sometimes even going deep), we shared some of our war stories. Mine were pathetic next to Jeff and Craig's. I could only muster up tales like breaking my Mother's nose with my baby sister's face, whereas they had incidents of stabbings, fractured elbows and, coincidentally, both had smashed and multiple shattered noses— Craig by a hockey stick and Jeff by a titanium lacrosse pole! I was cycling alongside them and had the perfect view of the outline of their uncannily similarly-shaped noses! Anyway, Jeff took the prize with his story which began:

"So one time at the ice-rink I got my balls split open…". Oh dear, I'm still struggling to recover from his gruesome tale, but there's a happy ending and he's back to full throttle. If you want the full story, you'll have to get it from the horse's mouth (no, that's not an oblique reference to his big ears again), so contact him directly for the full (painful) scoop…

Texas, Texas, you are so vast and it's only day 2 of our penetration into your cavernous belly. There are roads here which I suppose are very standard and common in that they are straight as an arrow for tens of miles—well, there's nothing like them in Europe. Trains sporadically passed by and, likewise, there's nothing like them in Europe, with carriage after carriage by the hundred all attached together, maybe a mile or two long. And be it the train drivers or the 18-wheelers on the interstate, many would honk or toot and wave us along encouragingly, probably thinking what daft nutters we were to be cycling along in the middle of nowhere, apparently on the way to nowhere.

We came across a pecan tree plantation that went on forever - yes literally - well almost. And lots of cows—as we know, Texans love their meat. As a vegetarian, Craig has been struggling enough so far already, but in Texas, you have to have sirloin steak in your cereal for breakfast. Actually, a new friend told us over supper that her husband had started a vegetarian club and actually received anonymous death threats on the phone, including the line, "We don't want the likes of you in this town!" We'd have to protect and look out for Craig—at least until we got to the meat-only restaurants and then he could wait outside!

Towards the end of the day we came across Simon Matthew ("Smat") and his little terrier, Raisin. Smat was cycling with a carriage in tow, which included a tent, belongings, cooking stuff, and Raisin's cage. They were homeward bound on a several-hundred-mile journey. He is a travel-writer/story-teller/journalist and we journeyed with him for a while at 6mph, enjoying slightly more erudite and enlightened conversation for a change after our puerile discussions à trois. The funny thing was that Smat said with Raisin in the cage, when dogs came to chase them down (our own perennial concern), the oncoming attacking dogs would get totally freaked out when the weird-looking moving bicycle-cum-carriage barked back at them!

The surreal experience of the day belonged hands down to Prada: we were cycling along that loooong straight road. There were no signs of humanity at all. And then, *in the middle of nowhere,* we came across an isolated one-roomed building with "PRADA" emblazoned across it, shoes and such like in the display window. It must have been a mirage. But we all saw it. And it really was there. Nuts.

At 105 miles we called it a day in a town called Valentine. We'd cycled past a number of ghost towns—dilapidated buildings of yesteryear—and this was another one, although apparently it has a population of 217. Well, I didn't see a single human being, but there was a truck parked outside a slightly rickety house. The ideal scenario would be that the owner of the house had internet access and would let us just park the Honey Badger outside, so that we could sleep there, get my blog posted and then depart from the same spot the next morning.

The alternative was a half hour drive to an RV park, which would mean that same half hour drive back the following morning, losing us precious time. So I plucked up the courage, walked slowly up the echoing steps to the front door, not with cowboy spurs but instead with clumsy cleats, and timidly knocked on the door, half expecting some wild-looking, eye-popping reclusive maniac to burst out bran-dishing a shot gun in my face. And sure enough he did! No, just kidding. Slightly anticlimactically, nobody answered. I'm sure the occupant had seen me, but as Craig observed, "There's a reason some people live in places like this: to get away from people like us!" Fair point. And any Texans reading this, sorry for reinforcing any negative stereotypes, you were the friendliest drivers of any State we've been through so far.

It was a very good day. Knees held, good mileage, fun chats, cooler weather, and no sewage problems. What more could a man ask for?

∞   DAY 12   ∞

HALLUCINOGENIC DRUGS FOR CYCLISTS

It was a pretty borrrrring day—at least the first half was. Overall, in crude terms, we did 86 miles at 13.6mph average from Valentine to Marathon (almost). We stayed at a basic RV park in Marfa with no showers or internet access, just electricity and water. In fact, consid-ering we drove 35 miles to get there, I'm not sure it was really worth it. So we got up at 5.15am and drove back to Valentine to start where we'd left off yesterday. On the way, as per usual, I phoned the family. In Josiah's lifetime (he's now two-years-old), he has not until now been able to talk to me. But now basic sentences are forming and this was my conversation with him: "Good morning, Josiah, how are you?" "I don't like you!" "OK, well what are you doing?" "Noth-ing." Game over. We usually do a bit better than that!

There was no love lost in Valentine. It truly didn't live up to its name. As mentioned, I never saw a living human there, either on Day 11 or the start of Day 12. It was just a rundown collection of ramshackle housing—that is, apart from one glaring exception, a big pristine sign for the local family and cosmetic dentist! It just looked so incongruous. The guy obviously made plenty of money to afford a nice sign by pulling everyone's teeth out, because some people in the area seem to have more fingers than teeth! Maybe his tools just consisted of pliers, hammer and chisel.

Part of the joy of doing this trip with Craig is that we are reminiscing about old university days and dredging up memories and names of people that had lain dormant for nearly two decades. I'd been thinking about my housemate Tommy's marijuana plants growing on his bedroom window sill (name changed because his Mum is a friend too and she's probably reading this!). I couldn't overtly destroy the plants, but I cared too much for Tommy's wellbeing, so I regularly urinated on them, hoping to kill them off. Sadly, I think that's the time they went through real growth spurts, so my strategy backfired.

I'd been there and done that on the drugs scene at school, getting busted on my last day by Dad, whose handling of this arrogant, petulant, combustible 18-year-old at a crisis point was treated with such deftness that it ranks right up there as one of his best parenting moments. If he'd barked angrily at me, I would have done the same back. But no, he just made me feel like a fool, and I remember resonating with his line: "Don't try to dredge up some spurious argument to justify yourself!" I didn't know what "spurious" meant, but I knew I was being an idiot, so I finished off my remaining gear the following afternoon ("Waste not, want not", as I thought) and haven't touched the stuff since July 1991! Why this random info? Read on…

We'd been advised to change our journey plans from the original Adventure Cycling Association Southern Tier Route, and this did cut out some mountains and save us 9 miles, but actually, as Jeff said:

"Next time we listen to someone's advice on directions, let's find out if they've driven the route by car or cycled it." You see, it was the worst stretch we'd been on. Miles after tens of miles of straight bumpy road. You wouldn't notice it in a car, but it was jarring with constant vibrations for us cyclists. We had to try to keep cycling on the white lane marker on the side of the road as that lick of paint probably took off 20% of the juddering.

But the hallucinogenic effect of staring relentlessly at that white line was the positive flip side to the negative tedium. Why don't you try it at home? If drugs are out of the question, as they now are for me, then this is a legitimate alternative. Paint a white line on the carpet, or draw one on the wall or ceiling, and just stare at it for two hours non-stop, maybe rotating your legs at a cadence of 60-90 turns per minute. Slowly you'll experience what we three today drifted in and out of. After three hours, wow! I could see a chicken jalfrezi on the horizon coming towards me, with Sag Aloo and Nan bread, followed by Twiglets, Doritos, an Ile Flottante, Nerds and After Eight mints, and then Lizzie beckoning me towards her, and then… I'll stop there.

When we had clawed back the 35 miles to Marfa, we stopped off at a Dairy Queen to get a milk shake and internet access to send my previous day's blog. Just then, another biker gang turned up, sending frissons up my spine after our experience a few days earlier getting run off the road. But these guys were a different breed, very friendly, middle-aged and just out for a ride to Tornillo. I chatted with a few of them, and then this one chap said, "You know, if your cycle had a motor on it, you'd go a whole lot faster!" Quick as a flash, when he heard what the biker had said, Jeff retorted, "And if your motorcycle didn't have a motor, you'd be a whole lot thinner." Then it all kicked off, forty of them against us three, so my two-year, pre-teen Judo stint stood me in good stead to hold my own in the pitch battle as ice-creams and milk-shakes were hurled across from rival tables. No, no, that was residual hallucination kicking in—they were far too nice for fisticuffs and sedately purred off again into the distance.

I'm glad to say that by now Jeff had joined the Bruised Buttock Brigade. I experienced a mixture of empathy and vicarious joy to know we were now in the same boat—that he was not bypassing this integral experience. The physical aspect of these endurance adventures is fascinating. Take Craig as a case study (so it's not always me moaning about my knees): he had a cracked rib, sunburnt hands, sore feet from his cleats wearing away, an aching backside, chafing wotsits, a dodgy gut, a burnt face, eye-problems from melting sun-cream dripping down from his forehead, a bruised head... but the great thing about the human body that I've observed is that you only really notice the one most painful thing. All the others, if they were at the top of the list of painfulness, you'd be moaning about, but they all pale into insignificance in comparison to the big one. "So Craig, are you OK?" I'd ask. "Yeah, yeah, OK, just got a sore arse!"

He'd wanted to stop off at the world-famous McDonald Observatory, but of course there simply wasn't time. It was named after William Johnson McDonald, who left one million dollars on his death in 1926 to the University of Texas for the construction of an observatory. Here was a good spot because it was high up (6809ft) and far from cities, meaning the night was very dark, unpolluted by lights or dust. The original telescope contains a mirror which can gather up 150,000 times as much light as the natural human eye and the Pyrex glass of the mirror was ground to one millionth of an inch accuracy and weighs three tons. It sounded interesting, but I still thought I'd prefer just to go to his namesake's for a Big Mac!

We came to Alpine and stopped off at the Honey Badger which was parked outside a fast-food joint. Jeff's bike was playing up again and needed dealing with. Craig went in to use their toilets and, would you believe it, was greeted by the town's only bike mechanic. I loved those coincidences! We went to his shop and he repaired the bike. Then we were back on the road. Craig had been complaining that his cleats were slipping out of the pedals, but he managed to fall over sideways again because he couldn't get them out in time—beautiful irony!

As we made our way towards Marathon, the weather turned. Lightning struck, there were a few twisters twisting a couple of hundred yards away, we experienced our first rainfall of the whole trip, and now we were cycling into a vicious headwind. Progress was slow. Then Craig's cleats died a death, so we had to call it a day, missing out on a few more miles. Fortunately it was no great loss because we were ahead of our schedule as it was.

So we headed back to Alpine for a superb evening at Liz's house. She was a "Warm Showers" host—the term for people who will take in cyclists and give them a place to wash and eat. We didn't know anything about her, but she was/is absolute class. After showering and making ourselves presentable, we scoffed loads of her delicious carb-rich fare whilst laughing with gusto as the banter flew between her (an Obama-loving staunch Democrat) and her boyfriend of fifteen years Mikey (an Obama-hating even more staunch Republican). What a fun and funny pair!

Such evenings are real highlights amidst all the hard grinding out of miles. Another guest called Albert had the same cleats as Craig and was willing to donate his so that we could continue early the next morning, rather than have to wait until shop opening hours, so that was another godsend. I would have loved to have more time with them, but we were dispatched to bed at 9.30pm by Liz herself— not to be argued with(!)—to get our beauty sleep (of which I needed much but didn't seem to be getting it, unlike all the others whom I had to bark at in the early hours of each new day to get them out of bed if we were to make it away in time).

∞ DAY 13 ∞
RELIGION, POLITICS, AND THE SADDEST ST. PATRICK'S DAY EVER!

At breakfast, Liz said she was going to join us on the first 12 miles of the ride, which was great because it meant we could have some more time with her. She will turn 60 this year, so was no spring chicken and feared she'd slow us down, but we were no speed merchants anyway and having others join us always added to the mix. We made it to our launch pad, got the bikes ready, and she promptly fell off as soon as she got on! I had just vomited up my breakfast, annoyingly, because I'd swallowed six pills in one go and they'd got stuck, then I'd gagged, hence the regurgitation. But those pills were precious, so I picked them out of the slightly fermented milky oatmeal mess and swallowed two at a time instead!

I would have loved to spend more time with Liz. If you hang out only with people who share your perspective on everything, then your views are just reinforced and never challenged. We had spent several days cycling along the Mexican border and she is a defence lawyer for those unfortunate Mexicans. She would speak with tears in her eyes about them, as I do about Burundians. Yet, in my experience, many people, particularly many from the Christian community here, have such dismissive, black and white views on immigration. So many of the drug mules who try to come over are forced to do so at gunpoint or their families are threatened. Once caught and sent back, they are killed on the spot if they don't immediately turn back around and try again. What would you do? So of course the situation is much more complex than we might think. There is so much desperation in the people who are willing to risk their lives crossing the desert to get to the "promised land"—and indeed many do die in the process. Clearly you could not have open borders because then the USA would be flooded with extra people and implode, but I have heard so many ugly comments about Mexicans from people who should know better, many of whom purport to follow a Saviour who was a refugee himself—it certainly challenges one's thinking.

We talked about other stuff as we pootled along. Her brother is a "Bible-thumping Christian", in her words, full of judgment and condemnation, most obviously because she is with Mike (a lovely bloke) whom she's not married to. Her brother, like so many others, is filled with intense hatred towards Obama and all things Democrat. So in hosting us, Liz knew from our website where we were coming from in terms of being people of faith, and was perhaps concerned that we'd be of a similar ilk (although not too concerned since she's very comfortable with who she is). She's been pleasantly surprised with us, I think, and said as much. It just made me sad that so many followers of Christ are complete turn-offs to people on the outside. We're meant to be all about grace, but often exhibit such a lack of it. There's a fascinating documentary on Netflix called: "Lord, save us from your followers". Obviously there are plenty of great models out there of authentic, sacrificial, loving, conciliatory followers of Christ (as we are trying to be), but still large numbers of religious bigots (perhaps more frequently from the hinterland, but by no means exclusively) mean we all get tarred with the same brush.

These comments are more US-specific. The scene in the UK is significantly different. Talking religion and politics as I just have is a sure way to alienate people in the USA, but God (if He exists) is not a Republican, he is not a Democrat, and those of us who say we follow Him have a self-imposed higher standard in terms of how we talk about, treat, and handle those who don't share our views. I could say so much more on this, but I'll stop there. Suffice to say, hanging out with Liz (and Mike and Albert the night before) was fabulously refreshing. Did we share the same view of the world? Absolutely not, but we didn't have to. She was a hoot. And in terms of going the extra mile(s)—literally!—of demonstrating kindness, generosity, hospitality, openness, etc, she was amazing.

Before we parted, Liz helped clear up the Prada mystery from the previous day. The Prada Marfa (as it's correctly called) was installed in 2005 at a cost of $80,000. The designers' intention was that it never be repaired, so it might slowly degrade back into the natural landscape. But three days after the sculpture was completed, vandals broke into the building and stole six handbags and fourteen right-footed shoes which were actual Prada products, picked out and provided by Miuccia Prada herself from the winter 2005 collection. The building was quickly repaired, repainted and restocked. The new Prada purses don't have bottoms and instead hide parts of a security system that alerts authorities if the bags are removed. So there you have it!

Mike was going to pick Liz up to take her back and sure enough, he drove past us near the end in a red truck. There's a very common sign around the State which reads: "Don't mess with Texas". Well, on the back of the truck was the sticker: "Don't mess with Texas women!" That's right, Mike, you didn't want to mess with Liz, we all agreed! We left her at Marathon, a small dying town which is really only sustained by an oil tycoon from Houston. With the wind at our backs, we hammered out 65 miles before lunch and all was rosy. We stopped in Sanderson for an interview with the local paper. All publicity is good for the cause, I guess. Then we pressed on into what turned out to be quite a nasty headwind. It's slightly soul-destroying to go down hills at 9mph that you should be doing

30mph down, but such was the fierceness of the gale, further shown by the fact that the wind was blowing rivulets of spittle out of my mouth!

At 4.31pm, four cars went past us in a row. Jeff said it must be rush hour—because in general we were so isolated and they were few and far between. He then had his head down as he chugged along and failed to see a rock in his path. His front wheel burst and at the same time his back tyre got a thorn in it. The double-puncture took a while to fix. In the meantime we'd told John to go ahead another 16 miles to the 100-mile mark. Back in the saddle, we pressed on. Every mile or so, our nostrils would fill with the acrid stench of rotting flesh and we'd look up to see the shrivelling carcass of a deer or a cow or a Havolina pig (the wild boar-like creature we saw earlier). Then Craig had a puncture and we had no more spare inner tubes.

We'd already reached the 105-mile mark by this stage, still into the fierce wind, but John had got his mile-markers wrong and was further ahead, plus there was no phone reception. We didn't know how much further he was. We expected to see him around each successive bend, but he wasn't there. It wasn't a big deal, but it highlights how much of a mental a game this is; those three miles were such a drain, expecting to be finished by then and having wanted to quit about 15 miles earlier. So, what with Craig's puncture, we had to wait to flag down a car when one eventually came past and ask them to tell John, whenever they came across him, that we were stranded some way back. As it happened, that didn't take long because he was actually just around the next bend out of sight!

I spoke to Lizzie who had just dropped off my folks at the airport to fly back to England. They'd been over to visit and help out whilst I was away, so now she would have three weeks to look after the gang by herself before my return. All the kids were sad and Zac (6) said: "This is the saddest St. Patrick's Day ever!" It was probably the first one he could remember, but it was a measure of how they were feeling. Josiah (2) had been a bit tricky in my absence and I was deeply aware that Lizzie and the kids were sacrificing a great deal for me to be doing this.

Tomorrow we would take a full day off, since we were ahead of schedule. We were happily and exhaustedly ensconced in Liz's second (or third or fourth) home—apparently things are so cheap here that houses cost about $40k. We smelt fresh after a lovely shower and Jeff had cracked open his "Anti Monkey-Butt Powder", if you can work out what that was for! Sanderson is so small that it doesn't have a single restaurant or bar, so I asked a local lady where people hang out on Sunday. She said at church and then at the ice-cream shop, so that became our plan.

∞ DAY 14 ∞
GAY FLORISTS AND CRIPPLING "DROUTHS"

So we had completed Week 2! In the last six days we'd covered 98 miles, then 109, 110, 105, 86, and 105, bringing the overall total to 1,227 miles—over a third of the way through. People who had ridden this Southern Tier route before us (most of whom took 10-30 more days to do it), had said that if you could get through the first two weeks without getting broken by it, then you were well on your way. So that was encouraging.

Since Day 14 was a rest day I forced myself to stay in bed until 8.30am. However, the honking freight trains going by from the early hours and Jeff's phone alarm clock going off every five minutes (which he'd plugged into the wall to recharge just out of reach until I roused myself) meant that it wasn't such a deep sleep. But hey, we were in a beautiful house with access to showers and a washing machine, etc, so no complaints.

I was due to speak at First Presbyterian. Before we went there, Jeff set up our GoPro Bike camera on the back porch on a ladder to film himself cutting his own hair. I don't think it was vanity, but it looked a little weird. He told me it was for David's documentary and he wanted to see the development on time lapse. I settled for that still-quite-weird explanation. Whatever, the freshly-shorn version of young Jeff was a definite improvement, although the sudden loss of hair didn't improve his hearing because we were discussing vegetables that are called different things in the UK compared to the US. Craig said, "What you call 'eggplant' we call 'aubergine'." Jeff said incredulously, "You call eggplant 'air-conditioning'?!" (Incidentally, old Geoff was making slow, but hopefully steady progress and would be flying into San Antonio to rejoin us on Thursday, but probably not in a cycling role any more. It would be great to have him back for the banter).

At First Presbyterian Pastor Toby had only been there a month and was the only full-time pastor in town. Sanderson has 850 inhabitants and was a lot busier in years gone by. But the ten-year drought in the '90s (pronounced "drouth" here, which sounds strange to our ears, but they must be correct—what do we know? They're the experts in drouths!), and a horrific train crash with a number of fatalities led to its apparent slow demise. Toby and his wife were great people and had a challenge on their plates. I shared my story and about our work in Burundi and Toby then preached briefly on the difference between a scarcity and an abundance mentality, which was excellent. The congregation numbered 25 and they were all extremely friendly. Many were ranchers (not farmers—there is a difference, cattle versus arable, and the distinction is an important one). I was corrected by someone because the former consider themselves superior to the latter. It hasn't really rained here for three years, so things have been tough. One old rancher who remembered the '50s drought (sorry, drouth), reckoned that these last three years were a shorter time-frame, but that the overall state of desperate dryness was worse than ever before in his experience. "How is your morale?" I asked. "Well, I don't know what I'd do without my faith. And it's all relative when I hear what you have to say about what's going on in Africa."

The only place to eat, so we thought, was the Dairy King. We headed off there, but it was shut. Next stop was the grocery store to see if we could buy a frozen pizza or something. The delightful lady there rang the Dairy King owners to ask why they weren't open, when they would open, etc, and spoke to them. Whatever the situation, they weren't opening. She then actually offered to make us pizza herself. What incredible kindness! Texans, from what we've seen, are just incredibly warm and generous people.

We declined as she was busy with other wannabe jilted Dairy King customers and drove past the flower shop, called 'Tis the Season, run by Buddy and Randy (US folk, you'll never have met an Englishman called Randy, because to us it means "sexually excited"—worth bearing in mind when naming your kids). John had a good chat with them and they were lovely. Not just lovely, in fact, but lovers to boot. When they moved there a few years ago (it being a very conservative small town), they anticipated some very strong reactions. But because they're so nice, so we've been told, there was a kind of collective denial: "They're not gay, they're just housemates!"

We picked up some food from the Stripes gas station and then caught up on emails and Skyped family back at church, as we had internet access there (which we hadn't expected this weekend). We got a lot of dull stuff done like bike maintenance, and washing pillow cases and towels. Generally it was so nice to have a break from the saddle (my butt was sending constant gratitude signals to my brain, quite the most lovely sensations you could imagine!), as we geared up for another torrid time over the next six days.

I worked late into the night to get as much GLO business out of the way as I could, in order to stay on top of things, which is an added pressure on this trip. As John and I finished and walked back home under the starry sky a family of five deer waltzed by and then the tree above us exploded into life as I guess we disturbed a hundred or so vultures from their sleep.

Earlier, over supper Jeff had asked: "Do you know the best thing I like about Simon?" Jeff had this boyish enthusiasm for everything, which was so very contagious and energizing. We had bonded over, amongst other things, a shared appreciation of our various butt-creams (mine is called Assos), like a pair of vintage wine connoisseurs, discussing the nuances of texture and aroma. But I was all for being encouraged, so when he posed the question my ears pricked up ready for some edification. I didn't expect what came next: "I love it that no matter what, every night if you look at Simon's ears, there's still a load of sun-cream in them!" Thanks bro. I took the compliment on the chin and then went off sheepishly to excavate every nook and cranny of my ears to remove the offending cream.

So the adventure continued. Tomorrow hopefully we'd be past Del Rio.

CHAPTER FOUR

IN THE BELLY OF THE BEAST

∞ DAY 15 ∞

HARD YARDS AND THAT MONDAY MORNING FEELING

The sun rises at about 8.00am here, so we were up at 6.45am. I was reconciled now with the fact that I needed, or at least got, three hours less sleep per night than the others. I wished I'd slept more, but at least it meant I had some early hours to commune and meditate alone. We showered, cleaned the house, and got away in time to start with the dawn, deeply grateful to Liz for two nights in her lovely house. I had realized the previous night (and the Sunday night before that) that I had that dreaded "Monday morning is approaching" feeling. I hadn't had it since before I went to Burundi and was in a marketing job in 1998. I used to drive back from friends in London on a Sunday night and think, "Oh no, another five days until the weekend!" Having it again now, in very different circumstances, made me deeply thankful that I've had fourteen years of doing something I love, which is incredibly energizing and life-giving. I guess many people hate their jobs and consequently hate Monday mornings. I don't take it for granted at all how blessed I am.

In terms of the Monday morning feeling on the ride, it highlighted for me just how much of this challenge is mental in nature, rather than physical. The physical is obvious, but actually we all agreed that the mental was harder. Getting up in the morning and grinding out another century—particularly on days like this when we knew the terrain would be dull and the weather was going to be against us—was a mixture of plain boring (hours of monotony), painful (chafing, bruised buttocks, knees, etc.), and exhausting.

I viewed things in weeks, so by Thursday I felt we were nearing the weekend, over the half way mark, and that was helpful. Of course, that didn't stop me enjoying the whole experience in general, which was a total blast, but it was definitely long, we missed our families a great deal, and it was still daunting as we approached the half-way mark.

On the team we all tended to have different jobs. Mine was to pump up the tyres each morning. I had this daily ritual of sticking the pump on, getting enough air in, and then yanking off the pump without catching my hand on the cogs. But I was such a muppet that with at least one in six of the wheels I would catch my finger on a cog and draw blood. Consequently, by this point my right hand had five scabs from such incidents. It was like providing a blood sacrifice each morning to appease the spirits of the wheels. It was a shame it didn't work, as we'd had a lot of punctures and would incur another three today.

Day 15 rewarded us with a tough, tough morning. The wind was right in our faces and progress was painfully slow. Craig's first puncture shredded his tyre—well, we tried blowing it up, but the hole in the wall of the tyre allowed an intriguing nipple-sized air pocket from the inner tube to squeeze out and when I touched it, the whole thing exploded. We had to flag down someone heading the other way to track down John in the Honey Badger a few miles further back, to come and bail us out with a new one. That ate a fair bit of time up and added pressure to our schedule. Meanwhile, some

Jehovah's Witnesses stopped by to attempt to meet our spiritual but not our physical need!

We came across the English family threesome yet again—they hadn't had a day off, had slept under a bridge, looked very much the worse for wear (the son was unaware of a bogey hanging out of his nose!), and were plain exhausted and fed up by the wind. They had been carrying their own stuff and journeying without a support vehicle, so all respect to them. It was a little soul-destroying. Going through the hills with the wind funnelled directly into us was like having a hairdryer in our faces. 48 painful miles were accrued by late lunch, during which I simply fell asleep through sheer exhaustion.

Craig is a real foodie, although he's a vegetarian—so I'm not entirely sure if those terms can be used together. (By the way, it's just a thought, but surely we didn't fight our way to the top of the food chain to be vegetarians?!) Craig had struggled with food on this adventure more than anything else, and since John was our cook as well as driver, Craig wanted to assume the role of culinary mentor to broaden John's range of offerings beyond spaghetti and tomato sauce. John seemed inclined to resist these advances and so recently we'd had the same offering to eat three days running. I wasn't complaining though. When you've half killed yourself for four straight hours in the face of an oncoming hairdryer, anything hot and moist tastes amazing.

I'll tell you a bit more about John. He was a brilliant asset to us cyclists, responding graciously and humorously to all our diverse requests for whatever. He had a slightly morbid fascination with the many objects of road-kill we came across on our daily travels. The previous day he'd been catching us up in the Honey Badger when he found one of those huge dead boars in the middle of the road. He swerved to miss it, but then decided to turn the Honey Badger around and go back to take a closer look. The Honey Badger guzzles gas, so that manoeuvre alone would have cost about $5! Later on that evening he treated us to a short film clip of the battered boar, focusing in on the nostrils that were still bubbling with froth—thanks John! Another intriguing element to John's make-up was his encyclopaedic knowledge of all things fast food. He could name any chain and then recite its produce, its market share and the calorie content—all in a slightly autistic Rain Man kind of way. Sorry for recording that fact dude! I say "dude" because John is a surfer dude from California, but he studied at the Citadel military school, an establishment not known for attracting surfers. Now he sported a very un-military bushy Jesus beard. All in all a fascinating combo.

We'd been warned there could be thunderstorms, flash floods and lightning, but that day the worst we had was a little distant thunder and rain. The rain was much-needed for the land and refreshing to us as it lessened the heat. In the afternoon, we really wanted to make it to a century, but weren't sure whether there would be enough day-light. We bloody-mindedly battled on, however, and finished with 112 miles under our belt, which gave us a great deal of satisfaction. We retired to a plush RV park which is apparently home to Texas' third largest swimming pool containing 1 million gallons of water (not that we had time to use it). We were welcomed there by a sign which read: "Howdy Trooper! Unsaddle and Rest!" That was indeed the plan.

We had a Skype call with Geoff, which had become a nightly routine. He would fly out to meet us in the next few days. We laughed our heads off because he shared how, when I visited him in hospital before he was flown out by helicopter to the specialist cardio unit in Palm Springs, he was pouring his heart out to me and said goodbye (in the "I'm on my way out" kind of way) and I (who as you may remember was struggling with lots of gut issues) dealt him a terrible stinker which he thought might finish him off on the spot, as well as the guy in the next cubicle! Incidentally, that hundred mile helicopter trip cost a cool $18,000 so we were grateful for insurance!

∞ DAY 16 ∞
CONTRASTING FLATULENCE

This was a fabulous day. We left Brackettville at dawn, so grateful after yesterday's killer session to have found an RV park with both showers and electricity. We got lost almost immediately and I hailed down a cowboy. He asked where we wanted to get to and I said, "Charleston, South Carolina!" in the tongue-in-cheek way I often did to see people's reaction. The English equivalent would be to flag someone down in Slough High Street and ask directions to Athens. Everyone I'd said it to—either because of my accent, or because their brains just could not compute such a crazy thought—had just ignored my answer and asked another question. When I said it to this cowboy and he grasped what we were doing, his eyes widened and he said, "Ohh mah Lo-r-r-rd! Gr-r-r-racious!" And, as we'd experienced before, these über-helpful people then wanted to map out our whole journey for us and went into incredible detail, eating up valuable minutes, when all we wanted to hear from them was that we'd overshot the previous left and just needed to head back, take a right, and go right again!

I was in a great mood as the weather was perfect, the scenery was becoming progressively more beautiful, and we'd burned off a load of extra miles yesterday so we were ahead of the game. This was always good for morale. John, however, was a little downcast. It was a lonely job being the driver and his job never stopped. He'd done well so far, but it was no doubt wearying for him. He needed company, so it would be great to have Geoff back soon. Craig was also subdued, missing his son Joel in particular (we both found that it was one particular child who seemed to feel more deeply the strain of our absence). It was tough to be away from family. Actually, each day leading up to 2.00pm, if Craig hadn't spoken to them back home by phone, he started sweating and hairs began to sprout on the palms of his hands, only receding if he got to talk to precious Beth and Joel before their bed-time. I totally understood him, he's a doting father and husband.

It's almost as if Craig has a gift of getting punctures—another four today. One tyre simply exploded, reminiscent of Burundi gun-fire. Maybe it was linked to his wearing a short-sleeved shirt for the first time. He made the decision because his only long-sleeved top had been worn too long without being washed and was pretty stinky and dirty, so it was a selfless call which received full endorsement from the rest of us. But you have to understand that Craig was pasty *white*. He was the shade of paleness you'll see every few hundred yards along the beach on the Costa del Sol in Spain every summer in Union Jack swimwear, which will give you a migraine after just ten minutes' exposure if you don't get your protective sunglasses on in time. He plied himself with sun-cream, and quite rightly too. I remember back in 1993 when we were in Brazil together working with street-kids and one night I sat with him through the early hours as he lay there horizontally rigid, in extreme pain, with silent tears pouring down his cheeks, no longer *white* but rather lobster *red* after too much time spent in the sun. Ironically, I was the one who fin-ished the day this time round with sunburnt legs after only using Factor 30 instead of the usual 50!

What's more, the day had now arrived when Craig has a cold sore ("cole sore" or is it "cold saw"? The 'spell check' function on my computer wants it to be coleslaw!). We didn't know when this would happen, only that it was inevitable. Oh dear, apparently herpes is very contagious and frequently spreads to different parts of the body. In the confines of the Honey Badger (I shared a double-bed with him), I didn't hold out much hope that I'd be able to steer clear and he helpfully told me that once you've got them, it's for life. Who needs enemies with mates like that?! We were very careful not to share toothpaste, bottles of water, etc. I had enough issues without adding "coleslaw" to my list of woes!

Craig is one of my most faithful friends. We'd take a bullet for each other. His name means "rock" and he is indeed rock solid and dependable. He treats me a bit like he's my mother, rolling his eyes a lot at my puerile antics and completely disassociating himself from my lavatorial humour. Speaking of which, Jeff asked him over supper why it was that he hadn't heard a single instance of flatulence coming from Craig's direction. Craig responded that it was because he only broke wind on the toilet. How well brought up is that?! Jeff replied, "Well that's why you've got a bleeding butt-hole!" Jeff is indeed incorrigible, but he was right—there are some things that shouldn't be stored up, they need to be let out!

I mention my puerile antics. The thing is, I spend so much of my life having to act very responsibly, maturely and (frankly sometimes) boringly that it's good to let off steam. In Burundi particularly I am high profile and can't let the side down in what is a very reserved culture. But it's not just there—in general, because of my role, I tend to have to behave myself for much of the time and can't totally let go of myself very often. I have the weight of providing for several hundred people on my shoulders, which is sometimes an overwhelming burden to bear. The joy of this trip was that I could really let what little hair I have left down. I felt like a dog let off a lead. That could be misconstrued as saying that I feel like I'm on a lead back home with Lizzie. Don't take it that way. If Lizzie's holding the lead, I love being yanked around! I wasn't totally switched off though. I was still leading this trip and so had to kick everyone out of bed in the morning and keep my finger on the pulse of things. But at the same time, because the lads are such low maintenance, I could enjoy just behaving like a big kid a lot of the time.

To redeem Jeff a little from the above comment, let me share some of his insights into flora and fauna. He studied environmental science for his degree, so had lots of very interesting titbits of information to give us. At one stage we went past a huge number of vultures enjoying some unfortunate rotting carcass. He proceeded to tell me that vultures urinate on their own feet, because the uric acid turns them white which reflects the heat and keeps them cooler. Furthermore, vultures don't just have an instinctive ability to seek out blood, but also oil. So oil prospectors used to follow vultures in the hopes of finding out where they might strike oil. Not a lot of people know that...

I'd done my own bit of research and planned to impress him at some stage with the following if we came across one: Texas's native horny toad is actually a lizard and can shoot blood from its eyes. Shame we wouldn't quite make it through Bracken Cave, near San Antonio, because it is home to about 20 million bats, which must be quite a sight. We'd come across some snakes so far, but no rattlesnakes as yet. Texas has fifteen different kinds of rattlesnakes.

So whereas both Craig and Jeff both knew a lot about flowers and plants, I knew virtually nothing. A lot of that day's joy came from seeing those multiple long thin green things, which we'd missed for the last week or more due to being in the desert. Yes, everywhere was suddenly so green. Parts of the landscape could have been Dartmoor or the South of France. After the desolation of the desert, the contrast was amazing. Maybe beauty has to do with contrast. The scenery was awe-inspiring after a week of sand, scrubland, cacti and rotting roadside deer. The long thin green things (grass) were such a welcome change. Jeff said, "Is this the prettiest place I've ever been in my life, or is it just because we've been in the desert for the last week?" I saw lovely *purplum flekidora explora* and golden dandelions (having not seen any flowers or colours for ages). It was a veritable sensual overload. Actually, speaking of contrast, only cyclists will be able to relate to the feelings of heightened euphoria when you transition from a bumpy road (which we'd been on for four hours, clenching tightly on the handlebars through the vibrations as we juddered along) to a smooooooth road. It honestly feels like holy ground. You want to jump off the saddle and kiss it. Contrast... very interesting.

We had no phone reception all day, being deep in the Boondocks. In one town(let) we came across a sign saying: "Great Food at the Boot 'n Buckles Bar & Grill"—real cowboy country. A father and son combination stopped for us when I flagged them down after yet another of Craig's punctures, to ask them to alert John further back along the road to bring a new tyre. They looked slightly odd. In fact, I said, "Hmm, those guys looked a little inbred, didn't they?" which was exactly what Jeff was about to say to me!

In an isolated field we saw umpteen old rusting geriatric tractors and other decrepit metallic farm instruments. There was a skilfully-soldered overhang with the words "Rust In Peace". Just past it, a border collie chased after me, and kept up with me at an impressive 20mph for 300yards before giving up the challenge. The other two were further back and it was my pleasure to see it then take them on, snapping at their heels. These dog attacks never ceased to make me laugh—at least after the event if I'd emerged unscathed—and watching Craig and Jeff struggle away as I looked back over my shoulder in hysterics meant I cycled off the side of the road and nearly came a cropper.

The new terrain was essentially rolling hills, which were forgiving in that you could work up enough speed on the downhills to get up most of the way on the uphills. Not all, however. We had our steepest climbs of the whole trip, which were exhausting, but also elating because of the surrounding beauty. Towards the end of the day, John went off to find an RV park for us. He was to find it, check in, come back to the main road and tell us whether we were staying there or not, and then we would come back to it. However, he missed it and drove on. So suddenly as dusk approached, we thought we'd lost each other. I approached a delightful farmer and he said I could use his internet. I imagined us trying to track John down through Facebook if he then managed to find some house where he could get on the internet. Remember, there was no phone access and it was extremely isolated.

In the end we decided to cycle on, thinking that as a last resort, we could return to the farmer and hopefully sleep on his floor and maybe have a fun evening with him, depending on how open he was to hosting three smelly, skin-tight Lycra-clad, dodgy-looking cyclists. But a few miles further up the road, that scenario was blown out of the water (actually a little to my disappointment, as it would have been a fascinating and unusual night which would have made a good story). There was the Honey Badger and around the back was John, cheesy grin on his face, lying in his hammock and reading his Kindle.

We'd made 108 miles and then settled for the night in Hunt, an obscure place where we were without water or wifi. Today had been probably the most enjoyable of the trip, and the irony was that we nearly missed it because we had been advised that we could use an alternative route and cut out the hills. That would have been tragic. Any ACA Southern Tier cyclists planning your own journey and reading this, make sure you go through Leakey, it is simply wonderful.

∞ DAY 17 ∞
LANCE ARMSTRONG AND THE CRASHING PUMPKINS

Lance Armstrong once said, "Pain is temporary; quitting lasts forever." Day 17 very nearly marked the end of my ride. What happened? Read on.

The day started early, as it always does, but especially due to my relative insomnia. Craig was so desperate to talk to his little Joel that he got up at 3.00am to catch him (in the UK) before he went to school. Such is Daddy's love, all the more because I know Craig really needs his sleep. Even as I had dosed, trying not to listen to him, I couldn't help thinking how moronic we Dads sound when we talk to our kids, putting on a 5-year-old voice and speaking to them slowly in a yodelling tone as if they're young exchange students from Korea.

We began with a long drive back to our starting point. It had been a bit of a waste, driving to an RV park without a shower or internet access, but we didn't know that was the case until we'd arrived late the previous night. The morning ride was beautiful. There were ranches along our route with imported exotic animals, including lions, zebras (not that we saw those two species) and plenty of emus and antelopes, which are always a beautiful sight as they leap effortlessly over bushes and rocks.

Interestingly (and I daresay there's a medical explanation for it), my mucus always liquefies in the early morning and needs to be constantly snotted out. There's no genteel way of getting rid of it (well, maybe Craig had devised one, but it was sure to be impractical) other than to cover one nostril and blow the other one clear, checking that nobody was following too closely behind. Well, suffice to say, I'd forgotten that cardinal rule a few times to both Jeff and Craig's chagrin. Being snotted on has actually been one of the most profound experiences of my life though, so I hope they can view the experience the same way I do—as truly life-changing. Let me explain:

After three years in Burundi, back in 2002, I was told to spend a year back in England to pre-empt burnout. So I did some further training (Anthropology, Development, Cultural Studies, etc.) at All Nations in Hertfordshire. During the summer term there'd been some social function and I was doing the washing up at the end. A certain young lady approached me and offered to help. I made some slightly provocative remark which she deflected so feistily that I was immediately intrigued. When the washing up was over, I whisked her off to the Jolly Fisherman pub, and we had two hours of incredible conversation. There was an electric connection. I'd never met anyone like her. Was she the one for me? Well, at one stage, I cracked a joke, which she laughed at. But (un)fortunately, her nose must have been blocked because she snotted across the table at me! It was then that I knew I had found my life-mate; that was the clincher! (For the record, Lizzie insists that it was only "vapour", so that you're not imagining Ghostbusters-style ectoplasm landing on my cheek. But whatever she maintains, it was wet, it flew across the table at me, and it sealed the deal). I don't know, maybe if you're struggling to form lasting relationships, it's an unorthodox method you might like to try? And lest you think it was a freak one-off event, Lizzie has managed to repeat the aforementioned "vapour" treatment on average about once a year since. Beware if you ever meet her and make her laugh!

The miles sped by through beautiful scenery during the morning. In fact it was our easiest day overall. It seemed a safe enough road, but a state police officer pulled us over and told us to be extra careful. There had been two cycling fatalities in the last month alone, which was rather sobering. Clearly the whole community was impacted because when I stopped off to ask at a hotel if I could use their wifi to send my previous day's blog, the kind clerk likewise immediately commented on it. We'd felt very safe on the roads thus far, spending very little time on busy sections, but we needed to remain vigilant at all times. One girl who set out from Charleston last year doing this route was killed by a big truck, and she was far from being the first.

On we journeyed. My mind went back to my first day at university and the first girl I met on the morning of our first lecture. We were both lost, but quickly established we were looking for the same room. It being Loughborough, England's sports university, we held the standard conversation on our sporting achievements. I told her that I was county-level squash, tennis, cricket, had won the nationals at rackets, blah blah blah, then said,

"And how about you?"

She said she was a runner.

"What level, county?"

"No."

"Regional?"

"No."

"National?"

"No."

"Well what then?"

"I'm world student champion."

She was (and still is) Paula Radcliffe, the current world record holder in the marathon. My sporting accomplishments looked very feeble all of a sudden. Why do I tell you that? Well, I've been thinking way too much about Paula these last few weeks and it's all because of Jeff. When Paula is running the final few hundred yards and she's exhausted, her head starts flapping from side to side. She's well known for it, and it may not look pretty, but it's certainly effective. Jeff cycles the same way. So whenever he's in front of me, which is several hours each day, I see his head bobbing up and down and side to side in a Southern Indian Stevie Wonder Radcliffesque kind of way. I tried to emulate him but it just didn't work for me.

Incidentally, on Paula, she was not just the best runner in the world but also a delightful lady, and extremely intelligent, getting a distinction in her degree. Some of the other girls on our course, however, had to find some weakness, and said in defiance: "Yeah, but have you seen her dance?!" What is it in human nature that always wants to drag people down…?!

We came across a mini-Stonehenge set-up. I hadn't read the guide books so didn't know what the deal was, but it looked almost as impressive as our Stonehenge in the UK (which isn't very impressive at all). I was dating an American girl a decade ago and when I picked her up from the airport I asked her what she wanted to see. She immediately said, "Stonehenge." I was flabbergasted. That wouldn't have come in my top thousand choices. They're just big, dull, grey, motionless, heavy rocks! But I guess it's the history, the five millennia, the mystique, which Americans clearly do not share on their continent to the same extent. Suffice to say, in this case, we didn't stop off to look at those big stones.

At the traffic lights, a man in a Mustang opened his window and asked me, "Are you Lance Armstrong?" I think he was serious, but the light turned green so I showed him I was by overtaking and doing 0 to 60 in 6.7 seconds. Well, Lance is a decent enough looker, isn't he? It's a first being likened to him. I usually get called Rick Mayall, Billy Idol (maybe when I had a full head of hair) or Paul Bettany. Around the next bend a charming lady dropped a big F-bomb on us: "Get the **** off the road!" Jeff just smiled and waved benignly. You couldn't ever really be angry with Jeff, he's just too nice. "She's not mad at us," he said, "she just needed someone to shout at." Glad to oblige!

During a loo break, it struck me how synchronized Jeff and I had become. Like ladies living together whose menstrual cycles slowly align, so we both need a wazz now at exactly the same time. I could tell within a minute of when he'd call out for a pee break and vice versa. Craig, meanwhile, similar to his output of flatulence, seemingly never went. It was a divine mystery. Jeff and I would stop sixteen times a day (twice hourly on the road) and Craig just waited there patiently for us to do our thang. One day, when we were in the mountains, far, far from civilization, we were taking a leak off the road to one side when a man drove past and beeped at us loudly, shaking his fist angrily. What was his problem? I mean, should we have bottled it and disposed of it at the next public lavatories 73 miles away? Or simply held it in for those several hours? Come on mate, you should try it yourself, give us a break!

Jeff's bike caused us more problems today, so we had some work to do on it when we returned to the Honey Badger. While that was happening I strummed on a guitar and sang the guys a song I wrote 17 years ago when I'd split up from a serious girlfriend. I'd played it to her at the time and we'd both cried. I'd hardly played it since, but for some reason did today. John guessed that it was a song by the Smashing Pumpkins, which I took as a huge compliment. So that day I'd been mistaken for both Lance Armstrong and the Smashing Pumpkins—that's got to go down as a good day in anyone's books.

But back to the ride. One road on our map was closed to vehicles, but we presumed we could get through. We soon found out the reason why. Around the next bend, the river had burst its borders and was cascading over the two lanes. We rang John to find an alternative route for the Honey Badger. John's phone had terrible reception, but we got through that time at least. Meanwhile, Jeff and I were excited at the prospect of wading through the river (you really couldn't tell how deep it was) carrying our bikes. Craig, though, started breathing heavily. He's not a good swimmer and feared being washed away. He needed some coaxing, but eventually agreed after Jeff did a trial run across, shoes and socks taken off and leggings hitched above the knees. It turned out to be not much more than ankle deep, which was a bit of an anti-climax, but our feet got a refreshing wash and were at their most sweet-smelling in weeks. Then, as we came up the other bank, an adolescent fruitcake in a beach buggy drove down to a ramp as fast as he could in the opposite field, before taking off, doing a backward somersault thirty feet high, and landing perfectly further down the slope. It was manifestly dangerous, and the dozen or so youngsters watching were whooping with delight and relief. We saw some official drinks sponsorship vehicle so maybe it was being filmed—who knows—but there was no ambulance or any such thing at the ready for what could easily have gone horribly wrong.

I took my first turn with the cue sheets and we promptly got lost, almost for the first time. These cue sheets have been crucial to us. Basically, every turn of the journey is planned (Turn Right on Main Street for 2.1miles, turn Left into Fifth Avenue for 0.3miles, etc.). These are thanks to Joe Turco, who slogged his guts out for many frustrating hours to get them done. I think he decided to put just one mistake on each page to keep us on our toes, and that's what I was blaming in this case.

It was always someone else's fault, but not this time. I'm just a muppet when it comes to directions. We needed John, but he wasn't responding to his phone. Pick it up, John, we don't want your voicemail! When we next saw him, he had five missed calls and somehow hadn't heard them. So the new advice was to put it on vibrate and leave it in his crotch. That way there was more chance he'd be stimulated into action. From then on, his strike rate at answering the phone improved remarkably!

So far I haven't mentioned a key cog in the Bike for Burundi wheel and that is Joe's wife, Bonnie. She had been my right-hand woman for the last eight months preparing for this adventure. Whilst we were cycling every day, she was beavering away back in Charleston, lining up speaking engagements, RV parks, press interviews, you name it. She did an amazing job and I was very grateful to her. Thanks Bonnie! She'd have liked to have been with us on the Honey Badger, I think, except that she'd have been exposed to a lot of unpleasant sights and smells as men constantly re-lubricated themselves with chamois cream and other such activities—not a pleasant experience, I assure you.

We were making great progress—which we needed to because of an evening speaking engagement 45 minutes away, meaning we had to finish in good time—until 3.40pm. We'd managed to hit 48.5mph down one hill on very juddering roads which made it feel a whole lot faster. In fact Craig (after his nine punctures in the last three days) actually thought his wheel was coming off and he was about to wipe out. I had just gone down a hill at maybe 35mph, and was coming back up when I changed down a gear. My chain somehow got stuck, jammed the derailleur, and in an instant the bike jack-knifed and I went sprawling onto the verge. I immediately thought I must have broken my wrists, because that is a classic injury from such a fall, and I certainly fell hard. But thankfully it was sideways and onto the grassy gravel as opposed to the concrete, so I was absolutely fine. In fact, I thanked God straight away, because I couldn't believe how little pain I felt after crashing out at such speed. Some pain kicked in after a few minutes, because I'd actually caught my crown jewels on the break lever as I went over the top! But quite honestly, as I wrote in the introduction, three kids is definitely enough, I've had the snip, and so any further negative impact downstairs is acceptable collateral damage.

We did 114 miles in total at just under 16mph average in seven hours. Then we drove to New Braunfels where I gave a talk at Northpoint, through a Burundi connection with some great folks called Brian and Sally. They fed us royally and then packed us off to a lovely Bed & Breakfast.

The day came to a wonderful conclusion as old Geoff re-joined us. The team felt complete again. And then at around 10pm we were having a steaming Jacuzzi together. We were all naked and Geoff arrived in a pair of very Bridget Jones-style knickers (don't be ashamed, Geoffrey), which we eventually coaxed off him—whereupon he set to washing them in the bubbles, saying, "They need a good scrub!" Welcome back Geoff!

∞ DAY 18 ∞
NO REGRETS

The great modern philosopher and sage, Jennifer Aniston, once declared: "There are no regrets in life, just lessons." It sounds profound at first, but actually on closer inspection it's really stupid, I think. Sorry to shoot you down, Jen, when you're not able to defend yourself (you would have been welcome to make a guest appearance though to lube my chain each day and fix my inner tubes)! But how could I/she/you not regret hurting people along the way, making mistakes that had negative repercussions on others' lives? That would make us hopelessly heartless and egotistical, which I'm sure Jen's not. There are lessons in life, but there are most certainly regrets too, surely?

Last night as we'd finished our ride, another lady called Jenny told us to use her driveway to turn the Honey Badger around, as we were on a dangerous road and it wasn't good to be stationed on the side of it. We got talking and actually she was possibly the first person we'd met who didn't think we were crazy for undertaking this adventure. The reason was that she was from Berkley, California, original hippy country, and back in the sixties at the height of the flower power season, her friends did a similar trip to us—but by foot! Yes, they walked all the way across the USA from West to East coast over nine months. She was 24-years-old at the time and had a job, so she chose not to take part, quite understandably. But that decision, fifty years on, constituted one of her biggest regrets.

So can we make a deal together, reader? I've lived this way for a long time now. I've messed up in the past. I've hurt former girl-friends (and have sought forgiveness from all of them wherever possible), so yes, I've had regrets. But can we choose to live in such a way that, as far as possible, we won't need to have any regrets? It's a state of mind towards living—an attitude that will shape us into recklessly generous people, endearingly spontaneous folks, risk-takers, adventurers, passionate for life and compassionate for others. Part of my life's mission statement has included the line: "Seek to live so as to get to the end of my life with no regrets." Sadly, however, most people's highest aspiration is to arrive safely at death.

The reason for such reflection is perhaps that I turned 39 today, and a birthday always provides opportunity for reflection, particularly one during which you're perched delicately on a razor blade for six hours straight. Yes, only six hours riding today, as this would be our speediest century so far and we had to stop because of another speaking engagement quite a long drive away in Austin.

I'm actually not really into birthdays. I can celebrate others' with gusto, but because I'm not into receiving presents (I'm honestly deeply content without extra unnecessary "stuff" cluttering up my life), I literally would not have noticed it today had the team not given me a card and several hundred messages come through on Facebook. Yet we have made it a point back in Burundi to encourage the celebration of birthdays, because life is such a tenuous gift out there. If 20% of babies don't make it to the age of five, then it's worth celebrating. And if life-expectancy is in the forties, then you'll rejoice at any grey hair that comes through on your head—it's a badge of honour! In fact, for some people, we make up a date for them, because they don't know the day they were born (many of the older ones don't even know the year), and we try to make it special for them, because life is hard enough as it is and it's good to spread a little love around.

There wasn't too much to report on the ride. The tornado warnings of a couple of days previously came to nothing. Actually, Jeff's Mum's friend, Karen, who lives near where we cycled past, had a studio in her back garden where she worked as an artist. A few years ago, a tornado struck, lifted the whole studio off the ground, then sucked her out of it. She regained consciousness almost a mile away with her studio close by. Quite a story! She's also made a donation to Bike for Burundi. Alison, if you're reading this, we're glad you're still alive! I presume with your second chance at life, you don't want to have any regrets either.

We averaged 16mph today, so it was our quickest so far. We came to a junction and a couple in a car in front of us were dithering, so we overtook them. A few hundred yards later, they drove up to us, opened the window, and hurled a tirade of abuse at us, pure bile. What makes people quite that angry? They were, thankfully, the exception. Texans had been wonderfully friendly and generous in our experience—although we rode past a farm gate which didn't look too inviting with the message emblazoned in spray paint: "Enter this property and you will be shot." I think I'm right in saying that Texan law allows you to shoot anyone on your property who shouldn't be there. But back to their generous nature: Karen, mentioned above, said she'd make a donation after our brief encounter yesterday and at a Shell station I spoke to Lynne who also said she would (just on the back of a 3-minute chat—although I'm not positive, since she seemed to think Africa was a country). Also, in Lynne's case I'd believe it when I saw her contribution on the website. I'd gone into the men's toilet just a few moments before Jeff (who was equally desperate, remember how in sync we were) and so he'd had to dash into the ladies' toilet, presuming nobody would be in it. There, however, he stumbled upon Lynne's little daughter—one minute ensconced on the throne enjoying a holy moment, the next shrieking for protection from this dodgy male intruder!

Drama struck at lunchtime. John pulled off the main road onto the grassy verge, which looked innocuous enough. However, the wheels sunk deep in the mud, and they were truly stuck. At this stage we cyclists didn't know what was going on. But with the wheels stuck, the Honey Badger wasn't as high off the ground, and my heart skipped a beat from a distance thinking it had turned on its side. Anyway, we ate lunch and a lovely African-American man pulled over to help. It's interesting that I felt the need to put his race in there, as I think about it. You see, I'm white, and just about everybody I hang out with is white—people in our neighbourhood, at the kids' school, at church, at the beach. In Africa I'm used to being the *only* white man around. Here in the US, although there were many people of other races, I'd hardly interacted with any of them. America remains a deeply segregated society. Hmm… So this guy called his friend (in the meantime we were off piling up the miles) who brought his tractor and had some difficulty but eventually managed to haul our precious Honey Badger back onto the road. Oof!

Our host in the evening was Michael Madison, a great guy I'd met in Burundi a few years back. He works for the Gazelle Foundation, a charity started by Burundian runner Gilbert Tuhabonye whose incredible story is documented in the book *This Voice in My Heart*. I'd long wanted to meet Gilbert, having read his story and knowing he was still very much involved in helping his home community in Burundi. Gilbert was one of a few known survivors of a massacre of Tutsi schoolchildren in 1993 when the genocide kicked in. About a hundred of them were herded into a service station and then set on fire. He hid under dead bodies for nearly eight hours and still has scars to show from those burns. Eventually he broke through a window with the bones of one of his classmates, bolting past the crowd of killers and managing to escape into the bushes in the dark of night. His book is well worth the read. We had a good chat. He looked stunned to see a white person speaking his language.

Michael had organized for me to give a talk after laying on some great food for us. Over supper, I asked our host, Dan, "So what do you do?" He answered: "I'm an engineer, I design chips." "Oh wow," I replied, "Jeff's Dad is a ship's captain." I was just too tired to concentrate! These evening talks, on top of the riding, were a real challenge physically, but I think people were moved. Craig lovingly encouraged me post-talk, saying I looked like the living dead! Everyone seemed to be out cutting the grass today, so I had the added nice touch of puffy, swollen, bloodshot, drugged-up eyes from the pollen. It was a struggle not to rub them. However, my discomfort paled into insignificance compared to Geoff. Having only just re-joined us he was in a really bad way again. He'd talked of leaving for England tomorrow, but said he may wait until Sunday when we would be in Houston. I didn't get to talk to him after my session because he'd already gone to bed.

Austin is an attractive city. It was founded in 1823 and is considered one of America's earliest "planned communities". Moses Austin, a St Louis banker, secured rights over the area from the Spanish authorities in 1820, but died shortly thereafter. His son, Stephen, took on the project and insisted that every incoming colonist had to present evidence that his character was "perfectly unblemished, that he is a moral and industrious man, and absolutely free from the vice of intoxication". By 1829 he was able to write, "You will be astonished to see all our houses with no other fastening than a wooden pin or door latch." Well, times have changed. The city's now huge and intoxication is most definitely no longer outlawed, let alone considered a vice.

Arriving at Dan's place, we had been met with an incredible treat: Michael had lined up for us the one and only gorgeous Georgie from "Austin Deep". As the name suggests, it's all about deep-tissue massage. Georgie seemed so kind and gentle on first impression, but once I lay prostrate on her spongy table, she turned into a butchering beast. I like to think I have a high pain threshold, but she had me grimacing, shrieking, moaning and groaning. I was putty in her hands. Had she threatened me, I'd have signed over my house (if I had one) or recanted my faith. It was excruciating and yet maybe somewhere deep down it was also a pleasure—I wasn't quite certain. Maybe I could process the event via some post-trip counselling. When I got up at the end, I could hardly walk. I felt like a boxer after fifteen rounds. I think I staggered to the shower, but can't remember really, as it was all a bit of a blur. I hope that's what I did because I came around to find myself undressed and lying on the bed. I hope I'm the one who did the undressing. I was also wondering whether I'd be able to even get up the next day at 6.00am, let alone cycle another hundred miles. Apparently this was exactly how I was supposed to feel, so… no regrets.

Day one at the launch on the beach in San Diego, having just dipped our bikes in the Pacific Ocean (Left to Right: Jeff Hennessy, Geoff Morris, Simon Guillebaud, and Craig Riley).

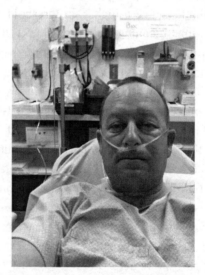

Geoff's tragic early exit, in the hospital in a bad way shortly before being medically evacuated by helicopter to a specialist cardiac unit in Palm Springs.

The trio on the open road. Hour after hour, mile after mile, day after day—sometimes fun, other times pure drudgery, but the goal of changing lives in Burundi always kept us pedaling onwards!

Bob McManus, his wife, and the donated bike – his spontaneous act of generosity as we walked past his yard sale meant that our ride was completed on time. Thanks Bob!

Leaving the Honey Badger after a break on the way up
the killer mountains in Tanto National Forest, Arizona.

Repairing yet another puncture in desolate Texas,
one of sixty seven in total on the whole trip.

Crossing the majestic mountains and plains of Arizona.

In Houston at the end of a long day, soaking our sore muscles in a Jacuzzi at our wonderful hosts, David and Rebecca Bearden.

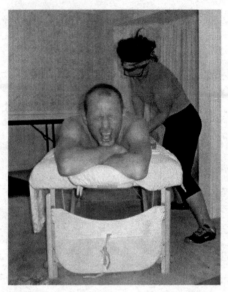

Shrieking in pain as Austin Deep's gorgeous Georgie shows
some tough love as she manhandles me on her massage table.

Good sport Sherry, holding the flag that I broke as
I crashed over her trailer in my dramatic accident!

Charging into the Atlantic Ocean on the Isle of Palms,
with John Stinson leading the way in acrobatic style.

Final celebratory team picture in our Superhero outfits, with Hadrian Hobbs
(far left) and Ron Banks (far right) who joined us for the last week.

CHAPTER FIVE

TRIUMPHING OVER TEXAS

∞ DAY 19 ∞

ANOTHER SAD, BAD DAY

Last night I only got a few hours sleep, as usual. My legs, post-Georgie, had screamed at me to stay horizontal, but at 6.00am we'd regrouped. Geoff came out and said he was feeling too rough to continue and needed to go back to England. He told us he couldn't put his family through any more of this and didn't want to be a further liability to the team. It was horrible and deeply sad. Geoff was the reason we were here. Bike for Burundi was his idea. His contribution had been massive, even without completing the ride—but that didn't make him feel any better after investing thousands of pounds and hundreds of hours in training and planning, as well as the general sacrifice involved for his whole family. It was gutting. We cried together, prayed together, and headed off, heavy-hearted, leaving him to seek a doctor's letter because British Airways wouldn't let him on the flight otherwise.

Frankly, I didn't want to ride that day. We drove to our starting point. I had a sticky phone call with Lizzie who was telling me off for staying up late writing my blog rather than getting much-needed sleep. If the human body is designed to recharge like a battery during sleeping hours, then my batteries were seriously low. I had a love/hate relationship with my blog. It was enjoyable sometimes, but a complete pain in the neck most of the time because I had to write it when feeling totally exhausted! But I saw it as an integral part of the deal in terms of thanking everyone who was supporting us for their contributions and to keep them up to speed. I loved the fact that so many people wrote in, telling me how they would read the blog to their family over breakfast and have a good chuckle, or read it on the train and burst out laughing, causing everyone to think they were weird. It was a great encouragement to me, but it did mean less sleep and the potential of incurring the wrath of the Missus! On this morning, the combination of sleep deprivation and having just said goodbye to Geoff made for more tears. When you're feeling low, you just want to be with your loved ones.

The day went fine. Due to just feeling sad, I suggested we only did 60 miles, particularly as we were way ahead of our schedule. But Craig was gentle and firm and so I did as I was told and was glad for it. We rode 106 miles in total. It was a late start because of the Geoff situation. I began with a puncture (I'd had one yesterday too), then the other Jeff's chain broke clean off, so that took a while to fix. We came across a couple on a tandem bike who were taking a photo outside the "Smallest Active Catholic Church in the World", so we invited them into the Honey Badger for a drink. They were spending several months wending their way across the States. The husband's business card read: "We're retired. Why hurry?" Good point. All this meant we had made little progress by noon, but we just persevered through until sundown.

This part of Texas was beautiful. It had a funky feel, going through little towns with random events taking place. There was Burton's Cotton Gin Festival and Warrenton's Antique Show, which was obviously going to start the next day and was massive, with mile after mile of marquees getting put up and displaying what looked like a load of rubbish. There were fields full of resplendent wildflowers. We were seeing the place at the best time of year. Apparently there were no rains at all the previous year, but seven inches fell just this week (hence the Honey Badger getting stuck in the mud yesterday), so people were happy with that and the fauna was blooming beautifully. A downside was that bugs were out in force and one of them flew into my (now puffy) eye at high speed, bouncing off my eyeball, presumably dead because half its body stayed behind.

Part of Bonnie's job was to line up places for us to stay and she liaised with John as he drove the Honey Badger. By 5.00pm today we didn't have anywhere to go yet. Sadly, my cousin Sharon and her husband Rohan were stuck with passport issues in India which meant they couldn't host us as planned. We stopped for a Coke at a diner. The waitress, Shannon, with a hugely enhanced pair of personalities, got us our drink and then came back quoting stuff from our website. She'd seen the Honey Badger's massive sticker in the car park and immediately gone online on her iPhone. The content had moved her. She was very helpful. I asked if she knew where we could stay and she hooked me up with a number. I rang, a German lady called Doris answered the phone, and it was the perfect fit. Twenty miles later we arrived at the designated shop where she would meet up in a rickety truck and guide us to her ranch. Her husband was a crazy man called Ernie, short in stature but larger than life. He'd built a vast hosting complex on his ranch because he loves people. There was a bar operating on an honour code (help yourself), animals (so Jeff and John went off to play with some calves!), and he had even built a stage to hold concerts. Not short of self-confidence, but not arrogant either, he said, "I'm full of ideas and the thing about me is, I make them happen!"

"You know, I made my first million, and I spent it," he continued, "so I made another million!" It's a shame we couldn't hang out together more, because I knew we'd have lots of fun with him.

Burundi was the country of the day today in *Operation World*, a daily prayer guide covering every nation on earth. Things aren't looking good there. The unions are calling on mass strikes, basic utility bills have quadrupled in price in the last three months, and I've just seen a report on the deepening corruption crisis. Most people are literally struggling to eat. We'll be back there as a family in a few months. I hope the peace will hold or so many more lives will suffer yet further.

Today Geoff posted a blog which included the following: "I have probably spent more time in tears of sadness than actual time spent pedalling. But, for each tear I have shed I pray it represented an orphan's life transformed in Burundi, Africa. If that's the case, then the ride, whatever it has thrown up, has been a total success…"

He was right, of course, but I was still gutted for him not to be able to completely fulfil his dream. Then it was time to try to get some sleep. As we lay down to rest we could hear the coyotes howling just a few hundred yards away. They sounded hideous, but it was all part of this very rich experience.

∞　DAY 20　∞

CRAZY ERNIE AND DISINTEGRATING BIKES

I remember a terrible film in the '80s called *Ernie Goes to Camp*. It was meant to be a comedy but was simply dire. The makers of that film should have spent some time with *this* Ernie, our host, because he is hi-la-rious. He's got ideas coming out of his ears and is like a little boy without a filter between his brain and his mouth. He knew we had to make an early start, so he arrived at dawn, bringing with him a few gifts. The conversation went like this (and to really get into it, for Ernie, you need to put on a deep full-bearded Texan accent):

Ernie: G'morning guys! I brought you a goose egg—ever seen a goose egg? Real big. And here, some Mexico Hill Ranch drinking mugs so you can promote me around the world. Do you want me to take you out in the truck to track down those howling coyotes? Oh no, actually, my truck's full of gear. My precious Friesian died last week—real sad—so I put her corpse out behind the shed and those coyotes are having a good time.

John: Thanks for the mugs. I bet you do T-shirts too!

Ernie: You're right! Hang on a minute… (goes off to fetch them, comes back a few minutes later). Here you go!

Simon: Do you ever take a break?

Ernie: You bet! I get in my truck and cruise wherever. I've got friends all over the world.

Simon: And Doris?

Ernie: Hell no! She's got to feed those damn cows—that's women's work, you see?! Those two donkeys over there—we wanted to see the birth real bad. We even went out during the night to watch their Momma. But Friday morning we came out the house and there was the first one, so he's called Friday. And then same thing Sunday morning, there the second one lay, so we called her Sunday.

And on and on he went, turbo-charged with energy, enthusiasm and vision for Mexico Hill Ranch. It was interesting because that's always been something that's struck me about the USA. Nobody does customer service like Americans. They are the best. They make you feel so valued and special. The French could learn a thing or two from them, and Burundians have taken customer *dis*service to another stratospheric level altogether (don't you love generalizations?!)—something we are trying to rectify with our own King's Conference Centre in Bujumbura. But Ernie was in a different league. It was pure service because he loves life, people, his ranch, his wife, and blessing others. So here's a plug to all Southern Tier cyclists: stop at Mexico Hill Ranch in Richards and stay a few days if you can, because you're sure to have reams of bloggable material and lots of laughs in the mix (I only spent a half hour with him)!

We feared not being able to get away from his enthusiastic clutches, but after a team photo like we'd been buddies for decades, they cheered us on our way, with Doris' parting shot: "Next time you want to wrestle cows, you know where to come!" Outside his home-made pub there was a plaque that read: "Some visitors are a blessing by their coming... and some are a blessing by their going!" I hope we were considered part of the former category.

On Ernie's comment about "women's work", I've got my own opinions. Women will only ever be equal to men when they can walk down the street completely bald and with a beer gut and still think they're sexy! (Before I left for the ride, I wrote thirty-five short letters to Lizzie, one for each day of my absence. Each note contained a funny one-liner, an encouraging verse and then a little personal lovey-dovey bit. The above was one of the one-liners!)

Back to the ride. We'd probably been through the worst now in terms of desolate wasteland, deserts and nasty mountain climbs. Today was 103 miles of pretty flat and easy terrain. But an easy day doesn't mean it was short on drama. Jeff's chain caused some problems (actually he was on the other Geoff's bike, because his own bike needed fixing as soon as possible), so we stopped off to work on that. He then smeared his upper lip with oil from the chain which made him look like he belonged in the Blue Oyster Bar—all the more with his effeminate Lycra leggings à la Village People singing YMCA. But then within a few miles, as I followed five yards behind him, we were beginning to go uphill when his bike jammed, he skidded, smoke came off the road, and he struggled to stay upright. We couldn't believe it when we looked down at his bike frame. It had snapped in four places. This was a $2,500 bike and it was totally wrecked, game over completely. Once we'd recovered from the shock, there was nothing else to do but change saddles, cleats, and get out our spare bike, the one Bob McManus gave us on a whim in LA the day before we started. Bob, if you're reading this, you can't imagine what a blessing you were! With Jeff's bike being out of action as well, and with us far from anywhere, Bob's bike meant total crisis averted.

It was pretty all day. We went past picturesque lakes with fishermen casting their lines in the still waters. We had shadows over us much of the time because of tall pine and gum trees lining the way. I nearly swallowed a butterfly as it flittered into my mouth. Craig had a ladybird (UK) or ladybug (USA) nestled on his arm for 60 miles. It must have been traumatized when it realized it was so far from home. Strangely, there were lots of crushed turtles strewn along the way and Craig rode over a live (now dead) snake whilst I had one rise to strike me as I flashed past ("flash" used in this context is to do with speed rather than nakedness. The team had withheld information from me yesterday because there had been an option to stay at an RV park whose dress code was "clothing optional", i.e. a nudist RV park. They thought that if they mentioned it, I would insist on staying there! But it was $100/night, which was prohibitively expensive. Maybe another time!)

We had two dog attacks. The first one was bizarre. I heard a lady shouting, "No Butter! No Butter!" and thought maybe it was just a case of a seriously vocal marital dispute on the contents of today's sandwiches. But the hollering became more heated and urgent. As I turned to look I could see this beast ("Ahhh, you must be Butter!") hurtling towards us. "She" (I didn't see any dangly bits, hence the educated split-second guess that it was a bitch) was half Alsatian, half Doberwoman and half lioness (I know that makes one and a half, but she was that big, mean-looking and fast.) We had a 300-yard head-start across their extended front lawn, but she nearly caught us. Phew!

The second one was traumatic for the sheer ugliness of the mutt that bounded towards us. Jeff said, "I didn't know we had hyenas in America." That's how ugly it was, but we were able to make a quick escape.

When you're riding for hours on end, your mind flits to all sorts of memories. When Jeff mentioned hyenas I thought of the time I was in Ethiopia in 1997 with twelve friends in a truck en route from England to Kenya. We drove three days solid across from Addis Ababa to Harar—all because of the Hyena Man. We tracked him down, having read about him in the Lonely Planet guide, and followed him to the extremities of the city. There we sat on the ground next to him at dusk as he hauntingly coaxed the ugly beasts out of the shadows of the city's rubbish dump, drawing them progressively nearer until they snatched morsels of meat from next to our feet and, even more exhilaratingly, from his lips as he unwaveringly dangled a piece before these instinctive killers. Nobody dared move, yet he seemed very relaxed. The tension in the air was palpable. We left him with a sense of reverent awe. But a few years later, a hyena worked out that he tasted even better than the meat dangling from his mouth, so he came to an ignominious end.

For some reason of all days this was the one we came across many other cyclists doing the same or at least a similar route to us. I so admired people who were attempting it solo, because it must be so lonely. There are pros and cons for doing it alone or in a group, but for us as a group, it meant constant company, banter, support, etc, and there was always the encouragement that one of the others had a more bruised backside, more extensive fungal growth, worse sunburn, a more throbbing headache, a stronger allergy or whatever than you!

We were really trying to save as much money as possible so that the maximum funds went to Burundi. So at lunchtime I enjoyed the same leftovers from New Braunfels for the third day running. It tasted so good. Anything tastes good when you're doing what we're doing. After lunch we had our only negative encounter of the day as a truck driver blasted past us and extended the long middle finger of fellowship. Then we came across a statue entitled "The Christ of Texas". The figure in question had extended arms and basically looked just like a clean-shaven Texan! It made me think back to my anthropology and Christology classes at All Nations where we observed how all cultures tended to make Christ in their own image. So you had a black Christ in Africa, a freedom-fighting Christ in Latin America, a Klu Klux Klan Christ, and so on—none of them the correct one. Sadly, whatever culture we come from, we're influenced and dragged away from the authentic Christ—the first century Jewish carpenter whose radical teachings, miracles, denunciations of the status quo etc., turned the world upside down and from whom our very calendar derives its dating. That Christ is definitely worth checking out in detail, if you haven't yet in any depth, and with integrity, because He might totally change how you see the world, as he has for me.

We knew we had a long drive at the end of the day to get to the other side of Houston, so we cranked out the miles. I felt comfortable for a while and I didn't think it was foolishness (because you tend to know how to manage your body post-injury), but I suddenly started to have those stabbing pains shooting from both knees which were reminiscent of when my dreaded injury first kicked in several months ago. Aaargh! Please, no! So we slowed down for the last stretch, completed the century and then drove two hours back to Katy, just outside Houston. I spoke to Geoff who had managed to talk his way into the British Airways VIP lounge during a long layover in Chicago and he said, "I don't even understand what's on the menu because the words are so posh, but it's great being in here!" He would arrive back in England the next day to convalesce with his family.

∞ DAY 21 ∞
END OF WEEK THREE

So on the evening of Day 20 we found ourselves in Katy, a suburb of Houston. After completing yesterday's ride, we'd had a two-hour drive here, since we had gone so far past our planned stop (wanting to get some contingency miles stored up in case of anything going wrong—and plenty had gone wrong so far to keep us on our toes). John brought up whether we should just stay at an RV park for the weekend to save on fuel (and I guess on his energy), but I thought having two nights in decent beds with hopefully some kind people and nice food was worth the drive. Well, the drive could have been the end of my trip. I was in the far back of the Honey Badger, lying down on the double-bed and catching up with some emails when John drove very slowly over a railway line. I guess there's a reason why it might be illegal to be in the back when travelling, because the leveraged bounce at the back from an unsuspecting dip in the road literally threw me five feet in the air, just missing the ceiling, with my laptop and ice-machine for my knees. It was cartoon-like, as if we were in space for a split second, before we all crashed back down. I hurt my back a little, feared that my laptop was bust, and took the hint to move up to the table nearer the front where minor bumps remain just that, minor bumps.

When we found our hosts in Katy, we knew it had been a good decision straight away. David and Rebecca were softly-spoken, incredibly generous folk. David had built up a very successful construction firm and wound it up in 2007, just before the economy went belly up. He was well-known as a man of integrity in the city— influential, connected, but beyond that simply a top-quality bloke. Their palatial seven-bedroom house was a sight for sore eyes and their Jacuzzi an incredible bonus for sore muscles. We ate together, had a swim, and went to bed very content.

Just to report on this last six days' mileage: we did 112 miles on Monday, then 108, 114, 102, 106 and 103—over a century every day, which was very satisfying. Week three was over and we had just two weeks to go. Our total was 1,868 miles so far in eighteen full cycling days.

Here's a bit of history on Houston and the surrounding area that was completely new to me: in 1835, Santa Anna became "El Presidente" in Mexico. He dissolved the Texas legislature (yes, Texas was a Mexican colony at the time) and sent troops northwards. Sam Houston, a former US Congressman, who had settled in Nacogdoches (where I spent some time about a decade ago when I was dating a lovely Texan lass), sent out posters further afield to recruit men for a ragtag resistance movement: "Volunteers from the US will receive liberal bounties of land... Come with a good rifle and come soon... Liberty or death! Down with the usurper!"

An early clash led to the hastily assembled Texan "army" defeating a Mexican garrison. Nobody quite knew what it was all about. As one of the colonists wrote: "I cannot remember that there was any distinct understanding as to the position we were to assume toward

Mexico. Some were for independence, some for the Constitution of 1824 and some for anything, just so it was a row. But we were ready to fight!" All that led up to the Alamo (which most of us have heard of, but frankly I knew virtually nothing about) where under two hundred Texans (and Tennessee frontiersman Davy Crockett) fought valiantly and held the fort against about three thousand Mexicans before being overrun and killed—all except fifteen women, children and servants.

Santa Anna's men pursued Sam Houston's army and eventually things came to a head near what is the modern-day city of Houston (that is one weird coincidence, did you spot that?). Houston (the man, not the city) rallied his troops with the cry: "Victory is certain! Trust in God and fear not! And remember the Alamo! Remember the Alamo!" Well, would you believe it, on the second day of skirmishes, those dopy Mexican officers took a very foolish siesta, just as the Texans wove through the tall grass until they reached point blank range. If ever the mantra was proved true, here it was: if you snooze, you lose! Within eighteen minutes, 630 Mexican soldiers were dead and 730 captured, compared to only nine Texan fatalities. The rest is history. It helps to understand a little more the strength of identity this State conjures up, particularly in its inhabitants.

I got a message from Michelle, Geoff's wife, to say that he was back safely in England having been upgraded on the BA flight across the Atlantic. Get well soon buddy! Basically, all the team except me were able to make today a complete day off. They had stuff to do like emails and downloading photos etc. Craig discovered that he'd been the victim of £6,000 worth of credit card fraud, which was the last thing he needed. The others lay in whilst I borrowed David's truck and headed across Houston's extraordinary spaghetti junction network of roads to give a talk at Clear Lake. Thank God for GPS because otherwise I'd still be out there somewhere looking for my destination. I had a great time with some folks there, before heading back to rejoin the team.

David and Rebecca returned from their church, Second Baptist Houston, which has, wait for it, 50,000 members. I kid you not! He's a deacon and was going to a deacon's meeting later on. I asked him how many deacons there were, expecting to hear a dozen or so. Guess how many there are? 800! I kid you not again! Craig was a member of a church in Luton which is considered big by England's standards with about 600 people, so he said incredulously, "They have more deacons than we have regular attendees!"

David invited us out to lunch at the prestigious Houstonian Country Club with friends of theirs, Jim and Bonnie. Jim, now a retired judge, had stood for Congress in 2008. He was a real character, as was Bonnie. So we had a gorgeous buffet in this plush venue with very impressive and successful people and we were all left wondering how this had come to be. We're just a bunch of sweaty cyclists crossing the USA! The connection that led to us hooking up was so tenuous and testimony to these folks' incredible generosity to host us random punters. Their son and daughter-in-law had worked for the Bush administration. She (Trish) as the President and First Lady's personal trainer!

Rebecca then kindly drove me across town again to another meeting which also went well. It did mean, however, that I spent about four hours driving that day and so didn't feel rested. Added to that was the fact that this was the main day to catch up on GLO business and emails. I was sorely hoping that as I went to sleep that evening I would accumulate some good hours in the bank, especially as were due to leave at 5.00am the next day. We had a team picture with David and Rebecca. I haven't told of all the gestures of generosity they made towards us, but suffice to say it was overwhelming and a real tonic to us in our battle-weariness.

One further funny anecdote to illustrate how superbly unique is this state and how strong is the sense of identity: I talked to Trish on the phone to thank her for hooking us up with her parents-in-law. It came out in conversation that when Trish was due to give birth to her first child, a son, David and Rebecca really wanted him to be born on Texan soil. Trish and her husband were living in Washington, DC, so it just wasn't going to happen. Instead, David and Rebecca sent up a mason jar of Texas soil to be put under the bed whilst Trish was delivering, so that it could honestly be said the baby was born over Texas soil! Furthermore, they got a signed certificate by the Governor, Rick Perry, declaring the baby an honorary Texan! Other car signs backing up those sentiments include: "I wasn't born in Texas, but I got here as fast as I could!", "I'm from Texas, what country are you from?" and "You may all go to Hell and I'll go to Texas" (Davy Crockett).

David, our videographer, had now rejoined us, having spent ten days away actually making some money for a living as opposed to working for us for nothing. We married men had agreed (or so we thought) with him before he'd left us that he'd maintain a solidarity abstinence pact whilst back home similar to the honourable Uriah, who refused King David's urgings to go home to his wife whilst his men were fighting at the front. Well, enough said. We forgave him because his documentary preview sample that he put together was stunning. It was great to have him back.

As I looked ahead to the coming week it was pretty daunting. In the last couple of days the temperature had ramped up significantly and particularly also the humidity. We would need to average 109 miles every day. There was no time for slip-ups. We just needed to churn out the miles. My knees gave me some real warnings at the end of yesterday's ride, so I couldn't push them as hard as I thought I could. But I'm thrilled to still be in the fight, so bring it on!

∞ DAY 22 ∞
THE LAST ACCEPTABLE PREJUDICE

Hoorah! At last, we're done with Texas. I'll refer to Texas as a she henceforth, not knowing if that's correct protocol. She is a staggering 5.3 times the size of England, to give you an idea of how McMassive she is (England is 50,356 square miles compared to Texas' 266,807, for those who like random stats). The privately-owned King Ranch in south Texas is bigger than the state of Rhode Island—another random fact for you.

We'd spent twelve days—more than a third of the whole trip—inside her. She'd played mind games with us, taunted us, heckled us, wooed us, and then opened her cavernous mouth wide to engulf us. She'd chewed on us, spat bits of us out, and then we slid helplessly down her oesophagus into her belly, where we were broken down before passing through her bowels and being pooped out the back end!

Oof! It felt good to be discharged, even if we were smelly as a result! Actually, we weren't because we'd landed at a cheap but clean RV park with good showers. We washed off the Texan dregs and perfumed ourselves with luxurious Louisiana RV-park-quality soap. I had a green tree frog stuck to the wall above my head ogling my ripped body throughout my douching, so as a punishment I caught him after multiple attempts and threw him onto Craig as he was showering in the next cubicle. I don't think either of them was very impressed by that!

So now we were in our fifth state and it was great to be there. By the way, as I reviewed our time in Texas, it was almost uniformly positive. The challenges of the desolate desert, strong winds, and multiple stinking rotting deer corpses made the latter, greener days all the more sweet. But above that, we met a whole load of wonderful people, so I will always have fond memories of that gargantuan state.

Our day started in Houston at 5.00am and with a tumultuous shock. John, aka Jesus-beardy man, had shaved it all off (and the whole Persian rug that covered his chest as well, but we won't go there). Well, he should have shaved it all off, but he actually left a tiny 'tache on his top lip. Remember Goose from Top Gun, Tom Cruise's co-pilot? That's our John. It looks *wrong*! I know the post-modern worldview rejects any kind of moral absolutes, but I'm sorry, this was wrong. I'll let you decide for yourself when you see the photos. To his credit, he was doing it for a joke (I hope) and I was meant to follow suit, but I just couldn't. After a week of not shaving I go strongly ginger and find it very itchy, quite apart from looking like an idiot, so I've never actually managed to grow a beard—which I wouldn't anyway, because I've inherited my father's prejudice against facial hair. Yes, it's the last acceptable prejudice to still hold on to. He told me once he'd never employ anyone with facial hair. Sorry chaps, shave it off and show me you've got nothing to hide! I do have a number of friends with louche slug-like growths on their top lip, so maybe now's the time to out myself as an anti-facial-hair bigot.

I could tell I'd had too much sun. We were out in it from 8.00am to 7.30pm. It was *hot*. It was *humid*. But we were hard as nails and ended up with our largest tally to date, a healthy 128 miles—which was great because it eased the pressure off our longest week. That time included a break for Craig to ring the Fraud Office in England to sort out his issues with someone filching £6k from his bank account. The hackers managed to change his address details, phone numbers, the lot—cheeky monkeys. We others were amazed at how chilled Craig was about this, but it turned out that because of the nature of his business it had happened a number of times before.

Jeff really struggled in the morning, which was a long one. We got 81 miles done from near Beaumont before our late lunch. He'd had a Chinese meal the previous night which wasn't agreeing with him and was also badly dehydrated. But after a few dollops of pasta, several lashings of Gatorade, and a nice call to his girlfriend Sarah, he bounced back to his usual enthusiastic and energetic self. Actually, he sometimes shows traits similar to crazy Ernie from a few days ago.

A family cycled past on two tandems, parents in the front of each with their two young sons (maybe 8 and 10-years-old). They'd been travelling for 22 days so far, camping everywhere—very impressive. We guessed that the boys were probably home-schooled because regular, over-stimulated kids would have gone stark raving mad with the monotony of so many eight-hour days in the saddle. Then we went past a church which had an electronic billboard which read: "Revival, 2012°Fahrenheit"—that's one smoking hot revival!

Then we came upon the most horrific sight. Now, let me tell you, we'd seen hundreds and hundreds of instances of road-kill in the last few weeks, from dogs to cats to cows to deer to skunks to armadillos, etc. But nothing compared to this unfortunate black Labrador that we sidled past, which had been mushed and literally split in two. We all let out a collective, spontaneous, repulsed "Yu-u-u-ck!" The stench, the sight, the flies... Next time you see a fly land on your sandwich, just think, it could have been inside a road-kill victim—but don't let that detract from your enjoyment!

What I thought was a temporary ban on my having the cue sheets and telling the others where to go had apparently been extended into permanence. My abject showing the other day, getting us lost as soon as I was entrusted with the task, led to Craig denying me any further opportunity to flex my map-reading muscles (which I pretended to be disappointed about, but actually that was my whole grand strategy in the first place!). I still managed to get lost alone today. I was too far ahead to hear the others shouting at me when I'd taken a wrong turn, so a few minutes later we contacted each other by phone—thankfully on this occasion there was a network connection.

I got the message that the people of Louisiana don't like litter. There were signs all along the roads, as with other states, but they were more punitive here. In California, the warnings were of a $2,000 fine, Texans settled for a $1,000 fine, but here it was a staggering $3,000 fine *and* community service. We'd be careful not to accidentally drop our empty Cliff Bar wrappers. Other interesting laws that I read about included the following (and obviously these laws exist because people have done such things in the past):

You could land in jail for twenty years for urinating in the city's water supply.

Stealing an alligator leads to a potential ten-year stint in prison.

There is a $500 fine for instructing a pizza delivery man to deliver a pizza to your friend without them knowing.

Running an abortion advertisement can land you in jail for a year.

It is illegal to rob a bank and then shoot at the bank teller with a water pistol.

Biting someone with your natural teeth is "simple assault", while biting someone with your false teeth is "aggravated assault".

It is illegal to gargle in public places.

It is illegal to shoot lasers at police officers.

Rituals that involve the ingestion of blood, urine, or faecal matter are not allowed.

Making a false promise can lead to a one-year prison sentence.

Every time a person is seriously burned, he must report the injury to the fire marshal.

Prisoners who hurt themselves could serve an additional two years in jail.

And finally, a state bill was introduced years ago in the House of Representatives that fixed a ceiling on haircuts for bald men at 25 cents!

A quick comment on mosquitoes—that's the most obvious new aspect I'd noticed in abundance here. Maybe it was because we were near a river, but there were gazillions of them and I hated the little blighters. There had obviously been lots of rain because we cycled past flooded areas with houses under water. Tonight we parked in Oberlin, Louisiana, next to a massive Casino, but were not even remotely tempted to venture inside.

CHAPTER SIX

THE CRASH

∞ DAY 23 ∞

CAJUN FATNESS

I might be emotionally unaware or insensitive, but had someone asked me yesterday about team dynamics and how things were going, I would have given an unequivocally glowing report about everything having been all sweetness and light amongst each one of us over the last three weeks. The fact is, with all of us extremely tired, living in close quarters, emitting copious quantities of noxious fumes, and not getting as much sleep as we would have liked, one would have expected a few decent humdinger rows by now.

Well, last night John asked me for a quiet word. He raised some issues that had been niggling him for some time. Most of them were very easily dealt with and arose out of misunderstandings and miscommunication. But if we hadn't addressed them, they would have led to resentment. So it was great that he did. I apologized for my shortcomings and that was that, nipped in the bud. Sorry there's no more salacious gossip or slander to share to spice up the narrative.

We had a late start because of having done so many miles the previous day and due to being in Louisiana's No.1 RV park for the princely sum of $20 for the night. From here on in, by the way, take it as a given that it's plain hot and humid.

So we were in Cajun country. Cajuns are descendants of French colonists in the 17th century who settled in Canada in a region they called "Acadia". They got a lot of rough treatment as France and Britain vied for supremacy in North America and eventually settled in Louisiana from 1785 onwards. Over time their new neighbours referred to them as "Cadian" which eventually became "Cajun". But if you have any association with the word, it's probably to do with cooking, popularized only from as recently as 1980 by French chef Paul Prudhomme when he created an instant classic with his blackened redfish. That's a brief summary in four sentences of what you could read in many books. I asked the lady at the Chevron station how she'd describe "Cajun":

"Hmm... let me see... it's road-kill food. They'll take anything, put lots of seasoning on it and eat the whole thang." No job for her then at the local Tourist Office!

We'd passed through towns with French names like Platteville and Moreauville (my sister Tracy's best friend when we lived in France as children was called Christine Moreau—maybe her ancestors?), so I asked how pervasive French still was. "My grandparents use it to talk to each other, but my generation and below don't speak it." Interesting.

The morning ride was full of fun and laughter. Having shared war stories last week, today we did Dr. Lurve stories, going through our past conquests and sharing some funny moments, as well as some more serious ones. I was relieved that all the girls I loved, spent any time with, and sometimes didn't handle very well, are now married to hopefully Mr Right as opposed to me. So my potential feelings of guilt could be assuaged and replaced with vicarious joy.

Over the last few days we'd cycled past many a mushed turtle, but today we came across a decent-sized living one, slowly clawing its way across the road. This was right up Jeff's street. He went into David Attenborough mode, picked it up (which prompted it to do a ginormous pee) and observed: "This is a red-eared slider, so-called because it has red ears and slides off surfaces easily." Craig, meanwhile, was getting hot under the collar at Jeff's perceived manhandling of the helpless turt: "OK, that's enough, let it go, leave it alone!"

"No, I'm just looking at it, it's not a big deal."

So I watched the hilarious interplay between Craig the tree-hugger's loving advocacy for the emotional rights of this unfortunate reptile and knowledgeable Jeff's rebuttal on the grounds that reptiles are amongst the lowest of the species with no feelings whatsoever. It might have come to fisticuffs and team schism, but the matter was settled with said turtle being put back down on the ground to go off on its traumatized way.

We passed lots of crayfish farms growing in rice paddy fields and came across some more road-kill. Jeff exclaimed, "Dude, look at that nasty jacked-up raccoon. Gnarrrrly!" Craig and I looked at each other, one of those quizzical acknowledgements that we can't possibly understand such US English. Then Craig corrected him: "The word 'gnarly' can only correctly be used in relation to trees!"

As we took a team leak, Jeff continued to educate us: "See those? They're Chinese popcorn trees. They require way too much water, then they grow fast, edge out the willows and dry out the wetlands. That one there is called a resurrection fern. See how shrivelled up it is? It can go without water for months and looks like it has died, but then springs to life immediately when the rains come." He's interesting, our Jeff. Actually, we now had a nickname for him. We needed one before when our other Geoff was with us, but never found one. Well, Jeff is just like Samwise Gamgee from Lord of the Rings—short, stocky, has big hairy feet, and is both very loyal and encouraging. Some might say the real Samwise is not the best looker, so let's not take it too far, but Jeff/Samwise is secure in his looks, so that's OK—unlike me at school when, for a while, the other kids called me "Yoda". I never liked that.

We went a little wrong today and did a few extra miles—which wasn't a bad thing because my mate Paul is sponsoring me $5/mile, so we might get lost a bit more often! We crossed over the 2,000-mile mark (that's $10k, Paul!), so things were going well. Entering Bunkie, we went past the Elementary School. It was recess and all the kids were out playing. I didn't see a single white face. A bunch of 9-ish-year-olds watched us over the gate and one called out: "We want to be dressed like y'all!" Maybe it was meant as an innocent compliment or maybe it was a barbed comment, but either way it provided further affirmation of how effeminate we look—that a little girl could want to wear our manly tights. Surely not!

Having aired one prejudice the previous day, I'll now confess to another. We came to a Shell station with a promotional offer: "Fat Tuesday—Premium Dairy Ice-Cream". Many of the people gathered there had girths at least three times the circumference of mine. We'd cycle past rotund folks rocking on their porches observing the scenery or texting away on their phones. Obesity is the pandemic of the 20th and 21st centuries and so many people here are simply texting too much whilst eating fatty Premium Dairy Ice-Cream. Come on people, get off your backsides and save your lives! Maybe it's easy for me as a skinny runt married to a skinny waif to say this, as it's clearly not one of my issues. But I met a skinny man at the weekend in Houston (the second worst city for obesity in the States) whose brother had just died weighing 500lbs (36 stone)! Tragic! And it's all the more a sign of how messed up the planet is when huge numbers of people in the West are dying of fatness, whilst tens of millions of people in places like Burundi are dying of thinness.

I sat next to a man on a plane to Chicago once. He was enormous. He snored so loudly that people several rows away caught my eye and rolled theirs. Three hours later he woke up and I said to him, somewhat nervously in case he punched me in the face with his supersized fist, "You know, I'm only saying this because I care, but if you don't shape up, you're going to die." He couldn't believe it! We actually had a really good chat, so if you want to accuse me of being fattist, then OK, but at least I'm a caring fattist! And Shawn, if you're reading this (which he could be as we exchanged details), I hope you're half the man you used to be.

Over lunch we were so wearied by the heat that both Samwise and I fell asleep. Craig was also quite dehydrated. His arm was so sore that he had neglected to drink, since it hurt him simply to reach down and pick up the bottle from his bicycle frame. But we had to keep going, so on we went. Samwise nearly got hit by a bus at one stage, maybe because his feet stuck out too far, but he's a nifty cyclist and weaved his way to safety.

We also had another dog attack. I reckon they win perhaps one in every thirty attacks and we were on about twenty-five so far, so we were due a defeat imminently. But all you can do in such a situation is to cycle faster than the bloke next to you and, if you do, you have the great pleasure of seeing their terror-struck eyes and watching their panic-stricken feet pedalling furiously away. Friendship only goes so far!

As the shadows lengthened and we came towards the end of the day, we passed by two isolated fields and suddenly there was a "whoosh" as thousands of birds darkened the sky—beautiful. We finished on 110 miles and they really felt hard-earned. It was a long slog. We checked into a nasty, cheap motel, easily the grimmest I'd seen in the USA—but at least there was hot water for a shower before bed.

∞ DAY 24 ∞
Lost in Louisiana!

Last night we'd booked just the one room so that we could take turns to have showers and then crash out, some in the Honey Badger and some in the dank, manky, musty room. At about 11.30pm, what sounded like a loud drunk started jabbering away on his telephone just outside our door. It went on for a while, so eventually I got up and went out to politely tell the guy to zip it. I found an Indian man, sat comfortably in a chair, talking Hindi with a total disregard for those of us trying to get some shut-eye. He got my message and quietened down. In the morning when I saw him again it turned out that he was the owner! I wondered how much repeat business he got if that's what he does every night...

We made an early start in the morning mist and soon crossed the majestic Mississippi River. If you take the Missouri as its main branch, the Mississippi is the world's longest river, measuring a staggering 4,300 miles, give or take. The levees to prevent flooding were absolutely massive, but levees certainly don't always work, as witnessed by Hurricane Katrina a few years ago. When the Mississippi does flood, it obviously destroys whichever crop is growing at that time, but people still like to farm that land because the sporadic flooding means the soil is very fertile. And as its purpose is simply to get to the Gulf coast by the shortest and steepest gradient, it regularly changes course, such that some towns have ended up suddenly in a very different position to where they thought they were. As Mark Twain wrote, "The town of Delta used to be two miles below Vicksburg; a recent cut-off has radically changed the position and Delta is now two miles above Vicksburg." (If any of this is wrong, it's Jeff/Samwise's fault—he's usually my source on these things).

At last we came across a live snake, albeit a very small one, after seeing so many dead ones littering the road, and according to Samwise it was a rough green snake. He could tell us anything and we'd believe him as it was his field of expertise, so we trusted him implicitly. It reminded me of a group of people from South Carolina that I once hosted in Burundi. We were up in the hills at a pygmy encampment and were going to sleep outside amongst them. I spoke in Kirundi to all the Burundians and told them just to play along with what I was about to do. I then told my US buddies that we were going to enact an intimate and profound pygmy custom. Due to the pygmies' close relationship with the earth as hunter gatherers, coupled with their awareness of how fleeting life is and how at any time they could return to the dust, when they received honoured guests, they would stand in a circle, grab some of the earth, spit on it, and then put it in the ear of the person to their right. This we all duly did in a deeply reverent and respectful way. It was very moving... until I admitted that I'd just made the whole thing up!

Louisiana is extremely green, but maybe that's just this time of year, I don't know. What I did notice is that a lot of people must have died here (or maybe people come to die here), because there seemed to be a plethora of cemeteries lining our route. Also, unlike every other state we've been through so far, this part of Louisiana doesn't have counties. Rather they're called parishes here—probably a Cajun thang.

We were really keen to catch an alligator (not to steal, we've seen how stiff the penalty for that is). David saw one but it quickly got back into the water. I'm not an expert on alligators, as I am on croco-diles, but I hope we do manage to find one. Most of my visitors to Burundi count it as one of their most memorable experiences when I take them to the Musée Vivant ("Living Museum"), where the old man in charge, Albert, gets paid an outrageously paltry $8/month. I always boost his wages with a tip, which means he then lets me do just about anything I like, including getting out the pythons, spitting cobras, mambas ("This one will kill you in two minutes, that one in ten", etc) and, even more excitingly, we enter into the cage with Lacoste or Romeo, respectively 39 and 27-year-old crocodiles. The bigger they are the slower they turn, so it's actually very safe to jump over the railing and yank their tales, which may not sound very kind but they always come back for more. One visitor, in panic when Romeo reared his head, turned around and ran straight into a tree! Where else in the world are zoos so interactive? That's one positive side to Burundi's lack of regulations!

Over lunch, I perused the internet on my iPhone to look at the latest international sport news and said to Craig, "Wow! Broad bowled Jayawardene on a no-ball when Sri Lanka were nine down, with him on twenty three and he went on to make sixty three for the tenth wicket partnership—so it'll be challenging for England on the last day, although they're two down for a hundred and eleven with Trott and Pietersen well-established at the crease, so you never know, but it'll take a fourth innings record for them to pull it off."

Samwise listened intently to what I'd just said and then spoke in bewilderment: "What in the *world* were you just talking about?!"

Welcome, USA friends, to the incomprehensibly mystifying language of cricket!

Meanwhile, Craig spoke to his little girl, Beth (7), who told him that she was sleeping on Daddy's pillow because of the comforting smell. Well, I don't sleep on his pillow, but I do share a double-bed with him most nights and I don't find his smell remotely comforting!

It was Craig and Samwise's chance to laugh at me in today's dog encounter. I normally ride at the front—not because I'm the fastest, actually because I'm the slowest, what with my dodgy knees, so I set the pace. Normally that means I can pull away the quickest from lateral attacks by grisly mongrels. This time, however, a boxer and a German shepherd were at my side before I had even spotted them. I was going too fast to be able to stop, but not fast enough to get away from them. So I pulled my left foot out of my cleat and started kicking frantically whilst waving my arm like a windmill and doing the loudest lion roar impression of my life. It worked. It was beautiful. I cheered with delight, relief and glee. Maybe I could get a patent to sell this to other cyclists? The other two had stopped way back. A few minutes later, Craig sidled up to me and said, with a totally deadpan expression on his face, "Very nice technique, Simon." These dog attacks are amongst the unexpected highlights of the trip for me.

Via the blog I'd had a number of people enquiring as to the current state of our derrières, citing a dearth of info on the topic of late. By this point, thankfully, most of our cheeks were chafe-free and, although still bruised, were acclimatizing to the regular rough treatment they endured on those razor blade saddles (particularly over Louisiana roads, which were the bumpiest so far). My Dad had reprimanded me for sharing too much information on bodily functions and such like, but I saw it as an integral component to the whole story. Speaking of which... one of our trip's greatest mysteries was the fact that Craig hardly ever took a leak whilst both Samwise and I did so frequently. I suspected that the three-litre Camelback device Craig strapped to his back and filled with "water" each day was actually a catheter, and that he disposed of the contents surreptitiously at each meal break via the Honey Badger's lavatory. Does that sound plausible? I'm not sure how else to explain it!

We were cruising along, into the eighty mile range, when things began to unravel. Samwise had had his second and then third puncture, so we'd run out of inner tubes and needed to call John to bring the Honey Badger. Samwise was a master tyre changer now, managing a change in just a few minutes, so he may have funny feet but he was fleet of finger. Once back on the road, we suddenly came to a dead-end. Something was wrong. The cue sheet didn't match up with the road. We got out the GPS and that didn't match up either. My iPhone has GPS on it too and that helped complete the picture. Some time way back before Clinton the cue sheet told us to go ten miles left when it should have been right. Doh! We were miles off track in the opposite direction.

We'd pushed hard all day because we were being hosted that night in Red Stick (Baton Rouge), which was a long drive away and so had needed to make good time. It was actually pretty impressive and surprising that this was the first time we'd got majorly lost. We'd overshot a road or two and taken a few wrong turnings, but usually we realized within a few hundred yards. The mood grew more sombre. Oh well, we just had to get caught up as much as possible. We reached the 100-mile mark and our usual "Hurrahs" were somewhat muted.

I'm not sure anyone else laughed, but I had a good chuckle to myself at how rubbish I am when it comes to all things flora and fauna. I saw a bird and in my mind said, "That's a kingfisher." Craig behind me said, "That's a beautiful heron." And Samwise behind him said, "Actually, that's a great egret!"

We finished on 105 miles having done an average of 16.2mph. Today we lost nearly twenty miles, which wasn't good. But when we started the trip, we were averaging an embarrassingly slow 13mph (before my injury it was around 19mph), so I was still just thrilled at our progress. Now we were heading into Baton Rouge for hopefully a fun and restful night with some more great people.

∞ DAY 25 ∞

SOLDIERING ON INTO MISSISSIPPI

Last night was spent in Baton Rouge with the delightful Dentons. As soon as we arrived there, we were grateful for having made the long drive to get to them because they were so generous and had prepared great food. Plus, having a hot shower, a comfortable bed and a massage chair is always a bonus. The downside was that the following morning we had to get up at 5.00am to make the long drive back to Easleyville and our departure point.

Some days are just a real struggle to get going on and this was one of those when it was hard to keep positive. We dozed in the car and arrived with the sunrise to start another long day. There was a thick fog so visibility was down to maybe two hundred yards, which made us as vulnerable on the road as at any time on this trip. Craig had these flashing bits that fit on either side of his rear tyre, so we were happy to have him at the back to take a hit if necessary! Off we rode, half-asleep, a generally heavy feeling hanging over us, exacerbated by the fact we got lost yesterday so had miles to make up. We had to choose to either wear sunshades, which misted up within seconds, or none, but then bugs landed in our eyes. I don't know if it was because we finished last night and then spent a long time all crammed into David's car (whilst leaving the Honey Badger at our starting location to save on fuel costs), but my knees were much worse today. It felt a bit like wading through porridge, not helped by the fact I belatedly discovered my back brake was rubbing on the wheel so I was having to put in an extra 20% effort!

It was always encouraging to talk to family on the phone. Both Zac and Grace's classes at school had a map on the wall and were plotting our progress across the USA. Jill, my physical therapist (as they're called in the USA, or 'physio' as people say in the UK) likewise had a map up in her studio as she, her staff and clients followed how we were getting along. It was all an added encouragement to know that people were lifting us up on days like these that were harder to get through.

We got honked at for taking a pee in the bushes. It happened often (getting honked at), so maybe I'd just got the wrong sense of what was OK and what was socially unacceptable. But we were miles from any houses, on an isolated road, and facing discreetly away from any rare passing traffic, so what was the problem? Are you on my side on this one? Whenever we got beeped at, I always thought back to an incident in Ethiopia back in 1997 on our expedition to Kenya:

On arrival in the sprawling capital, Addis Ababa, we had just the one contact address, but no directions. I desperately needed to relieve myself and was encamped on the front roof of the truck with my mate David, watching from above as cars and people bustled all around. For an hour we went to and fro, getting contradictory directions from literally dozens of people. I couldn't wait any longer and was wondering what emergency contingency plan I could concoct. At some traffic lights, for the umpteenth time we asked for directions. Below me was an open gate and a rare plot of grass. I saw my chance. I jumped off the top of the truck and told David to let the others inside know that I was doing important business, so that they would wait for me. I darted through the gate and began relieving myself in an attractive flower bed. Immediately, two soldiers and a ferocious Alsatian came running, all three of them barking at me: "Stop! Stop!" I looked over at them, then down at what I was doing, and then back at them, facially gesturing that I simply couldn't comply just yet with their wishes. They understood that, so instead went to lock the gate, which now seemed much bigger and more foreboding than before. What's more, I could see the truck beginning to pull away. It was my turn to shout "Stop! Stop!" Yet again I was desperate, but now for a different reason. Fortunately David heard and the truck pulled over. But now I was locked within the compound. I was finished by this stage and came over and tried to shake the soldiers' hands. For some strange reason they didn't want to! They were furious, seething, sweating profusely, trembling, snarling, muttering away in Amharic, which I obviously could not understand. "I am so, so sorry. It was a mistake. Please forgive me." Time stood still. It felt like an eternity, but finally they reluctantly opened the gates in response to my shameless grovelling and I gratefully rejoined the truck. It was then that I made the discovery that I had just urinated on the front lawn of the Ministry of Immigration! I believe I was blacklisted and will never be allowed to enter the country again!

We came across a copperhead snake in the road. It had been run over but was still alive, so we had to be careful as they are venomous. Jeff and I were all excited about it and I took a photo of Jeff with his grinning face as close to it as he felt safe, with Craig saying, "Leave it alone! What are you doing? Why are you doing this?" Then I put the poor thing out of its misery. More dog attacks followed, but I'm now only recounting new ones if there's a distinctive twist in the tale (tail). Actually, one little Chihuahua came running towards us bleating pathetically, which reminded me of my friends Sarah and Jean who were returning by car to San Antonio after a week's break in Mexico. Shortly before the border they saw a miserable Chihuahua, much the worse for wear, lying in a drainage ditch next to where they'd parked. They felt sorry for the wretched mutt, so they hid it in their car, crossed the border and took it home with them. Sarah grew so quickly attached to it that she actually allowed it to sleep in bed with her that night, before taking it to the vet in the morning. It was then she discovered that it wasn't a Chihuahua at all. Rather it was a Mexican desert rat with rabies!

(OK, that's not a true story, it's an urban legend, but today was pretty dull and I did think of that story when the pathetic Chihuahua came running towards us!)

We stopped for lunch just as Jeff's back wheel gave him renewed problems with a spoke breaking off. It took quite a while to sort out. After food, we got back on the road only for him to have a puncture after two minutes and then another one two minutes after that. The poor guy was really fed up (which is why he's back to being Jeff—I don't think on reflection that he enjoyed being called Samwise), but only for a few minutes because he's probably the most jovial man on the planet. We had to wait for the Honey Badger to show up again and I lay down on the warm tarmac for a breather, only to find that the next I knew of it was when I woke up and everything had been sorted out—a reflection of how exhausted I was.

The last forty miles were difficult for me with my knees telling me they'd long had enough. By this stage we were in Mississippi, our sixth state, having passed through Bogalusa. Most houses seemed to be pre-fabricated portacabins from what we'd seen so far. Mississippi is the poorest state of all and people don't seem to have many positive things to say about it. We soldiered on until we'd completed 112 miles, meeting Craig's parents shortly before we finished, as they'd flown out to be a part of the latter stages of our adventure. Then we were hosted by Steve and Tania and their forty-six cats and dogs in a place called Poplarville, "the Blueberry Capital of Mississippi"!

They really put in a special effort to line up an authentic Mississippi meal for us with crawfish, which you eat by yanking bits off and slurping the flesh. As I'm allergic to them, I just watched the others try to eat them with zero finesse as it seemed a sophisticated art. I'm sure my hosts would have liked me to partake, but I would have barfed (my favourite US word) all over the table, so it was good that I refrained. Tania said she'd like to do some work overseas, "...so long as I can take my donkey with me!" They were very different from Ernie at Mexico Hill Ranch from a few nights ago, but unique in their own way, which is part of the joy of hooking up with new people who all have a different story. Sadly, I felt too out of it to really engage and stay up late talking, which certainly would have been entertaining.

A few laws still on the books in Mississippi include:

If you sire two illegitimate children, you will go to jail for at least one month.

It is illegal to teach others what polygamy is.

A man may not seduce a woman by lying and claiming he will marry her.

Private citizens may personally arrest any person that disturbs a church service.

Cattle-rustling is punishable by hanging.

Horses are not to be housed within fifty feet of any road.

∞   DAY 26   ∞

MAN DOWN... AND IT'S PAINFULLY NEARLY OVER FOR ME

It only takes one second to have an accident. Life is full of small margins. I would not forget today in a hurry.

Today marked a big event for my family—my parents' 44th wedding anniversary. I'm so grateful to them for all they've been and done for me throughout my life. Great long-lasting marriages might be becoming few and far between, but I'm deeply thankful to be a product of one.

In terms of morale, I think yesterday represented my biggest battle so far, which meant that I found it a real effort to write anything on the blog. Steve and Tania were fascinating people. They were a bit like Richard Briers and Felicity Kendall in *The Good Life*. Apparently, I misrepresented them by recording the fact that they own forty-six cats and dogs. The true facts are: they have four dogs, seven cats, four goats, ten chickens and two mules (hence the comment about only going to serve overseas if she could take her donkey with her). They'd laid out home-brewed beer for us and the other guest for the evening—a delightfully rambunctious guy called Paul, who had obviously been sampling it repeatedly before we arrived, because I don't think we got the fully sober version. It made for great entertainment. He'd brought along an array of instruments as he was part of a Mississippi gospel blues band and wanted me to join him on the guitar, but I just had nothing left in my tank. Another time.

Steve, originally from New York, worked for the State Department. I asked Tania what line of work she was in. She replied, "Simon, I'm a glorified butt-wiper! I tell you, there's no glamour in caring for old people." Steve confessed to being a socialist (a cuss/swear word in these parts that could get you lynched!) as he observed the brokenness of the state. He talked of the local high school and how they promoted abstinence rather than teaching kids about birth control and, consequently, the teenage pregnancy rate was terribly high. Because it's a Republican state, taxes are low, so there are very few programs that can be funded. This means it lags behind as literally the last state on most indices of good things and the first state on most indices of bad things. Hence, a socialist agenda with increased taxation would surely benefit here. I hope I'm representing your argument well, Steve, if you're reading this!

We were woken up in the early hours by the sound of multiple cocks blasting their mouths off. Apparently a lot of them are reared here for cock-fighting, although it is illegal. We got up and Steve and Tania sent us off after a superb breakfast of pancakes and strawberries, which was a huge fillip for morale. Then back we drove to our starting point. On the way, I listened to a voice-message from my gorgeous children, saying they loved me and missed me. Again, in my tired state it brought tears to my eyes, but we hadn't got too long to go now.

We managed to get off to an early start. It was humid enough that I was already dripping with sweat by the time I'd checked and pumped up our six tyres. And then fifteen miles into our ride, the unthinkable happened.

We saw a middle-aged lady cycling alone (the first on our whole journey, as women normally go about as least in pairs for safety reasons). I rode up alongside her and we got chatting. Her name was Sherry. She'd actually started from Austin with another lady but the latter's work rate wasn't up to speed so they'd gone their separate ways. Sherry was obviously packing in the miles whilst pulling a trailer cart containing all her belongings. She'd cycled all over the US. Funnily enough, two of her recent cycling buddies had decided to become vegans whilst on the ride. The Southern states are not the time or place to decide to become vegan, what with their penchant for all things meat and fried! She told me her Dad's funeral was happening today, in just a couple of hours. He had died, aged 76, of cancer, but had insisted she continue her ride, as he was an adventurer himself. She was obviously upset, but a real trooper, and I could tell she was glad for a little company.

She then asked me what we were doing. I told her about our fundraising efforts for Burundi and reached into my back pocket to get out a card from the zip-lock plastic bag where I kept my iPhone. We gave one to anyone and everyone we came across with the Bike for Burundi website details and a little about us. We were cycling along slowly in parallel as I did this. When I handed her the card, with my left hand holding the right side of the handlebars and the zip-lock bag, I suddenly totally lost control and veered sharply away from her in an arc to the left into the other lane. I thought I'd wipe out then, but somehow managed to just about regain control and veered back towards her in an opposite arc to the right.

There's a hilarious YouTube clip of a Dad going down a slide with his daughter on his lap and their momentum keeps him going at the bottom as he stumbles forward literally another twenty steps, almost able to regain balance but actually eventually totally wiping out on his head. Well, in slow motion it was like that for me. I thought I'd been able to steady myself, but in the moment I was a complete moronic nincompoop. You see, I was still one-handed, because my brain didn't tell my hand that I could let go of that stupid, insignificant, three-by-five inch card, of which we had about six thousand in the Honey Badger anyway! As I careered back towards Sherry, I could hear the others' gasps behind me and see Sherry's scared eyes pleading for me not to take her down. But I duly smashed into the back of her bike and trailer. My legs flew off and I was upside down, my bike somersaulting, and I landed badly on the verge beyond her. Meanwhile, Craig behind me was taken out by my upturned bicycle and likewise came crashing down.

The scene was one of total devastation, in sharp contrast to the bucolic peaceful countryside around us. I was down and my back was damaged. Craig was down and he was nursing bruises. I'd snapped off Sherry's trailer flag (an eye-catching warning to vehicles). An alternative title for this section could have been "Hitting the Sherry"! As with my previous crash, once we realized it wasn't too serious, we all burst out laughing. I felt such a muppet. It had been so spectacularly uncoordinated of me, and it could so easily have been game over. My back was definitely bruised, but I would be fine.

I apologised profusely to Sherry and we got some duct tape to fix her flag back on. She asked us to pray for the funeral as we were going on our way, so we prayed with her there and then: "Lord, thanks for the chance to bump into Sherry today!" I prayed for her and for the funeral due to begin an hour later and we parted. I looked forward to reading her own blog to see how she recorded our encounter.

David, our film-maker, was in sight filming us, but was pretty sure he had the wrong camera rolling at the time. Oh, how good it would have been to capture the incident live, I thought! We left Sherry and the next twenty minutes were spent in hysterics as we relived the incident. It was that nervous-relief-elation kind of laughter. Jeff said: "That was the best fall I've ever seen!" More laughter. He piped up again: "I've spent so much energy laughing I need to eat another Cliff Bar!" And as we finished the morning and pulled up to the Honey Badger for our standard second breakfast, after two lovely hours of cycling, I said: "That was probably the best morning of our trip," to which he replied: "Yes, and all at your expense."

We got into the Honey Badger for a second round of pancakes and David uploaded the film he'd shot. And, whadda ya know, the genius had managed to shoot it! The camera was stuck on the back of his car, held in place by a sophisticated network of bungee cords, and was just rolling away. But, beautifully, you could see the whole crash until the end when I fell over, off camera. But you can still catch my bike going upside down and, if you look really carefully, see Craig wiping out as well. To view it, visit www.bikeforburundi.com Enjoy it, it gets funnier with repeated viewings as you see how each of us is impacted!

When David showed it to us, you would have loved to have been a fly on the wall inside our Honey Badger. We were lying sprawled across the tables, sofa and floor, laughing our heads off for several minutes on end. In fact, I haven't laughed that hard in years, literally. I was sweating from laughing. All of us, except Craig, who was munching on his breakfast. We looked at him and asked: "Don't you find it funny?" He said, "Yes, very funny, I laughed at the time, but now it's time to eat!" My back was bruised, but my tummy was aching from that time. Beautiful.

We got back on the road and I think I had so much laughing juice pumping through my body that I didn't talk to the others for the next fifty miles, just occasionally cracking up to myself. It was a gorgeous day of cycling, going along straight colonnade-style roads lined with trees to offer shade. The trees had obviously been the victims of a "controlled burn" because of their black trunks. It's a way of preventing devastating forest fires by setting an area ablaze so that all the accumulated fallen leaves and twigs on the ground are burnt off under close supervision and then the fire is put out, thus making the spread of any future fire less likely. Actually, we had a decent downpour of rain which doubled the fifteen minutes of rain we'd had all trip.

The sign outside Magnolia Baptist read: "Is your life running on empty? Free fill-ups inside." I was low on Gatorade by that stage and could have done with a refill, but it was shut. The floodwaters were really high with some houses submerged as we entered Alabama (our seventh state) and turtles would regularly slide off rocks into the water as we passed them by.

After 82 miles we had a serious issue. Craig's right arm had been giving him problems for days. It had got to the stage where he couldn't feel three of his fingers at all and he could barely use his whole arm, just resting it on the handlebars and mainly using his other one. He's a suffer-in-silence tough nut, but he pulled up in trouble, so we knew it was bad. I rang my superstar physical therapist, Jill, back in Charleston, who picked up the phone straightaway, thankfully, and diagnosed him down the line. She gave him some exercises which immediately brought some relief. It sounded like a trapped nerve in his neck, so hopefully with those exercises he would get back to full strength soon. He'd had some tough days with other (well-documented!) body parts, but maybe this afternoon was his toughest.

It was great to reach Mobile (for UKers, pronounced "Mo-beel"). We cranked out 110 miles at 16.1mph, going past a few trashed houses from previous hurricanes. Smelling the sea air and hearing the seagulls was so encouraging, and seeing the beautiful Portersville Bay brought further joy and satisfaction. It wasn't the Atlantic Ocean yet, but we were getting a whole lot closer. We passed where Forrest Gump captained his shrimp boat and then came across a sign outside a few lower grade houses which stated "Beware of Pit-Bull with AIDS". Hmm… that's the equivalent of the welcome to the Texan farm that had: "If you step on this land, you will be shot!" But surely the Mobile police weren't so totally relaxed about AIDS-ridden psychopathic pit-bulls roaming free, were they? I didn't believe the sign, but neither was I tempted to go any closer.

We drove to Daphne to stay the night in the home of a family who were out of town. After showering, we were hosted by Ken and Ceil a few streets away, who picked us up and dropped us off at the end. It was a feast, prepared by a real foodie. We had lots of fun with the different accents. In fact, the first thing I asked Ken was: "Do you know Rob Sturdy?" He seemed a bit non-plussed: "Do I keep a rope steady?!" We've got two new team members who have just flown in from Charleston on Ron's company airplane, so Ron's the new daddy of the trip at 49-years-old, and Hadrian is a final-year student from the UK but studying in Charleston, preparing for an iron man event in two months. We had a lovely evening with incredible food and fun people. Then it was back to bed and a little sleep before a very early start. It had been a long one, but hey, it was one seriously memorable day. Man down... but not out!

CHAPTER SEVEN

SWELLING MEMBERS

∞ DAY 27 ∞

BOTCHED ROMANTIC TEENAGE LUNGES!

We had a 5.30am start in order to get to the ferry which is part of the ACA Southern Tier Route. It had been lashing down with rain throughout the night and so we had our first grim, drizzly cycling session, but only for 8 miles until we came to the ferry terminal. As it was raining, we sheltered underneath a house on stilts. A woman called Janet was doing likewise, so we got talking, and she ended up crying with me over her wayward son. We prayed together, I gave her a hug, she said she'd get on our website and make a donation, and off we went again on our way. Just before getting on the ferry, I gave another man a card, and he said he would look us up too. Then it happened again with another man, who was the shuttle driver (more on him later). Through these and many other encounters throughout our trip it has struck me how Americans (particularly those in the South) are so much more open, friendly and less cynical than British folk (speaking as one myself). It's actually normal here to have a really positive interaction with strangers. Whereas back in the UK if someone unfamiliar is too friendly, most people are so wary that they keep their eyes down and get past them as soon as possible.

The ride across the bay was just 5 miles, but it knocked many more off the journey and meant that we had a lovely coastal cycle ride for most of the rest of the day. John finally got rid of the louche slug on his top lip by shaving it off into the sea! We were now a squeaky clean fully-shaven crew.

On we cycled when we reached terra firma at the far end. Having new blood on the ride in the form of Ron and Hadrian was great. They had more energy with their fresh legs and provided different things to talk about. I love Ron to bits. He is a recovering alcoholic (been dry fifteen years) and a successful man, but what is so endearing about people who have been through AA is that they are incredibly honest and real. They've learnt that they can't survive if they fake it. So, as always with Ron, it was straight into meaty chats with lashings of good humour thrown in as well. And what with him being new, he was super-enthusiastic about accosting passers-by with our cards, which led to a "widow's-mite" contribution of $5 from one poor fellow, a funny interchange at an intersection with a biker in the other lane as we delayed the traffic fumbling to get a card to him with the light now green, and more.

I get sent news on Burundi every day by Google Alerts and today something positive came through. It wasn't the usual massacre, disease, refugee, AIDS, famine, corruption stuff; it was altogether more encouraging, albeit slightly random (but we'll take anything positive we can get from Burundi!). I quote:

"A long-fingered frog last seen in 1949 and feared extinct has come out of hiding in the forests of Burundi, a small country in eastern Africa, scientists reported this week. Called the Bururi long-fingered frog (Cardioglossa cyaneospila), the amphibian is about 1.5 inches long, with a black and bluish-gray coloration. They knew the individual discovered was a male, because only the males of this species sport a 'ring finger', one extra-long digit on each foot with spines running along it; scientists aren't sure what this lengthy digit is used for."

Back on the road, a spunky brown-and-white Jack Russell chased us for 500 yards at incredible speed, barking himself hoarse. Bearing in mind each of his four legs must have been about 8 inches long, that would have been the equivalent of several miles for us. He just wouldn't give up! He reminded me of our old dog, Benson (both he and Harley have died in the last few months after 16 years as the Guillebaud family dogs), likewise spunky, brown-and-white, and a Jack Russell. We used to take Harley and Benson into Burnham Beeches for long walks and another regular walker was a lady with five huge Alsatian bitches. Benson, all of twelve inches tall, would see those bitches from half a mile away and wham, he was off! He charged into battle, totally confident that he could tear them all apart, the other woman screaming a warning that he would get munched in one mouthful. It took him years to learn, often the hard way with blood drawn, that he wasn't quite as big as he thought he was. But I loved his heart! Oh for more of us to enter life's fray with such fearlessness! So, Harley and Benson, RIP! (Actually one of our two dogs in Burundi has also died—we called them Stark and Naked, so only Naked's left now!)

Our short sojourn in Alabama came abruptly to an end, like so many of my romantic teenage summer escapades, lasting less than twenty-fours hours after one blundering lunge too many! Every single Alabamic human encounter was a positive one, but as with those halcyon days of youth, there were plenty more fish in the sea (so to speak), or states in the union, so our fickle fealty flipped and flopped to Florida, our eighth state.

The roads were a lot busier than we'd largely been used to because the coastal area was more densely populated. It was dazzling in its beauty, so Craig's double-puncture wasn't as dull an experience as it might have been, since we had the mesmerizing view across Pensacola Bay for consolation. We finished our 112 miles in good time, the new boys seemingly handling it fine, and headed back into Pensacola for an unexpected treat. David and Rebecca, our last weekend's hosts, had paid for us to have two King-sized bedrooms at the Hampton Inn for two nights. Wow! We love you D and R! So we grabbed a quick shower and headed out for a Mexican meal and then back to bed, extre-e-e-emely grateful for a day off the next day to rest our weary limbs. For some reason, Craig didn't want to share the massive double mattress with me tonight and had made up the sofa bed to sleep there—his loss! I checked my email before switching off the light and got this message:

"Simon, my name is Terry Etherton and I am the shuttle bus driver on Dauphin Island. I tracked you down on Facebook. Hope you guys had a safe trip today. Just wanted to let you know that Sherry was at the Ferry landing this afternoon. As we were talking I showed her the card you gave me and she was telling me about your accident. I told her that you had uploaded the film of it to your site. She was going to check it out. Be safe and glad we met."

Sherry, do get in touch—and watch the YouTube clip, it's superb!

∞   DAY 28   ∞
REST

Oof! We were nearing the home straight. Last week saw us complete 128 miles on Monday, then 110, 105, 112, 110, and 112, bringing the total up to 2,549 miles so far in twenty-four cycling days. There were under six hundred to go and I couldn't wait to be back home with Lizzie and the children. I honestly couldn't believe I was still in it and was absolutely delighted that my knees had held firm and that nothing too serious had gone wrong to jeopardize the whole trip (apart from, of course, Geoff's devastating exit).

Today was a full rest day. Our bodies were telling us about new areas of aches and pains. We couldn't afford to know about them during the relentless weekdays, but now that we were taking a little break, they were piping up with various complaints!

One wonders how the following laws came about, but take a look at what still stands on Florida's statutes:

The state constitution allows for freedom of speech, a trial by jury, and pregnant pigs to not be confined in cages.

Women may be fined for falling asleep under a hair dryer, as can the salon owner.

A special law prohibits unmarried women from parachuting on Sunday or she shall risk arrest, fine, and/or jailing.

If an elephant is left tied to a parking meter, the parking fee has to be paid just as it would for a vehicle.

It is illegal for a doctor to ask a patient whether they own a gun.

Doors of all public buildings must open outwards.

It is illegal to sell your children.

It is illegal to sing in a public place while attired in a swimsuit.

Men may not be seen publicly in any kind of strapless gown.

Having sexual relations with a porcupine is illegal.

It is considered an offense to shower naked.

You are not allowed to break more than three dishes per day, or chip the edges of more than four cups and/or saucers.

Last night we decided to go and visit Brownsville Assemblies of God church. I'd heard about it years ago. It's where the Pensacola Revival took place. From 1998 to 2005 they had around 5,500 people show up just about every night, as people got healed of blindness, cancer etc., and so people came from all over the world to witness and be a part of it. They had approximately two and a half million visitors from all over the USA as well as overseas during that time. Since we were in Pensacola, I thought it'd be a shame not to check it out.

We immediately went into the wrong building on the campus where the kids' work was taking place and a strapping big African American guy called Robert quickly intercepted this gang of six suspicious-looking men. Having ascertained that we were actually kosher, he pointed us to the main auditorium, a 2,500-seater. He was a real character and went to the head honcho to tell him about us, so it meant we got introduced to the whole congregation during the service. Afterwards we chatted more and heard how by 2.00pm each day during those earlier years, people would camp out in a line that stretched around the block to make sure they got into the evening meeting. I was glad we went, although I fell asleep during the sermon. But then again, I was so tired that I would have fallen asleep during just about anything, except another of those deep tissue massages like we had in Austin!

Then it was back to the hotel, where I cracked on with emails, GLO business, logistical stuff, and then we went to the cinema to see *The Hunger Games*. I've read the book and the film does it justice. The apocalyptic scenario depicted is a horrific one and yet is one that many Burundians are actually already living as their daily reality— starvation, crippling poverty and hopelessness. In fact I'd just received a report from Kirundo in the North of Burundi of seventy-six people starving to death this month. The life expectancy of the pygmies we work with was just 27 before we got involved, by providing them with clean water, teaching them farming methodologies, building them a school and more. Twenty-seven years—that blows my mind—but wonderfully things are changing and this trip means that they'll change further. So what more motivation do we need to press on through the pain when it gets hard?

∞ DAY 29 ∞
SALIVATION, SWEAT AND STUTTERING

We scoffed lots of food at 6.00am at our Hampton Inn before heading out on this last week of our epic adventure. The sun blazed down on us all day, which was mostly spent on Highway 10 from Pensacola to Marianna, where I eventually checked into a grotty room at the inappropriately named "Executive Inn Motel". There was absolutely nothing "executive" about it. The others were in an RV park a couple of miles away, but we had three more guys joining our crew late that night, driving up from Orlando, so we needed to meet them somewhere and this seemed like a suitably smelly establishment to initiate them into the non-glamorous world of Bike for Burundi!

This was by far our speediest day on the road. Several factors were at play: it was easy terrain and we had a mild tailwind helping us along, but most importantly, Craig's family were waiting for him further down the road. Craig is normally very chilled out, but in fifteen years of marriage he had never, until this trip, spent more than a night away from his wife Emma, and then when the kids arrived from Beth (7) and Joel (5). So he was on a mission, he was focused and he was cool, calm and collected, as he blasted off at silly speed expecting us to keep up with him. I had two punctures in the first hour, which slightly put a spanner in the works. We retired my back tyre after the second one—it had served me well over several thousand miles, but was breaking up a little and we needed to press on towards Craig's prize. After thirty days of separation, he was just desperate to be reunited with his family and reacquainted with his wife—though not necessarily in that order!

At one stage we went past Cortez Street, which reminded me of a man by that same name who landed at Vera Cruz in 1529 to begin his conquest of Mexico with a small force of seven hundred men. He purposely set fire to his fleet of eleven ships once they had disembarked. So his men on the shore watched their only means of retreat sink to the bottom of the Gulf of Mexico. With retreat no longer an option, there was only one direction in which to move: forward into the Mexican interior to meet whatever might come their way. Sometimes we need to take similarly drastic action in life or else we might go back to our old ways, settle for the easy option, and short-change ourselves of new, enlarged experiences. Hmm… Hey, maybe that's a random thought, but you try sitting on a bicycle for six hours (our shortest day) and see if your mind doesn't wander off on tangents!

We'd covered 84 miles by lunch at the giddy speed (by our standards) of 17.8mph. Emma and kids and her Dad had flown out yesterday to Atlanta and driven down and were just a few miles away. Craig was positively salivating, sweating and stuttering in anticipation. It only took a few more miles back on the road and there they were in Chipley, waiting for Daddy with a big banner. Precious little Joel, most affected by Craig's absence, was über-excited and it was a joy to see them all embrace. The excitement continued for the kids as they got to ride in the Honey Badger with all its fascinating gadgets. I didn't check with John, but I wondered whether he was more or less keen to have children after an hour's close exposure to the junior Rileys!

In no time we'd finished our 106 miles and Craig fickly abandoned us in a flash to go and spend the night with his family. What was that about?! I was confused by his twisted loyalties and hoped it didn't undermine team unity for the rest of the trip(!). We headed to an RV park, sweaty as ever, and jumped into a lovely section of a stream (called "the blue hole") which was freezing, but deeply refreshing and invigorating. The mosquitoes were out in force, which slightly marred the experience, but it was a bonus treat at the end of another century ride, our fourteenth in a row.

So Brannon, Jeremy and Marcus would be with us in a few hours, which I was excited about—more fresh legs in the mix—but not excited enough to wait up for them. I needed some beauty sleep.

∞   DAY 30   ∞
BOXERS REVEALING TOO MUCH... TIMES TWO!

I forgot to mention an important detail about last night's dip in the stream, which was Ron's transparent, white boxer shorts. When we leapt into "the blue hole" at the RV campsite, Ron jumped in along with the rest of us, but when he got out to jump again the poor teenage girls who were also there voted with their feet by fast deserting the area. Ron was beautifully unaware and liberated, beaming with enjoyment and satisfaction at a long hard day's cycling completed. You get the picture. We decided to leave poor Ron in the dark over that one, since we didn't expect it to happen again! But then I later discovered that these weren't just any boxer shorts—they were "Royal Highnies". Here's what their promotional material says about them:

"Once upon a highnie,

It began as a quest to create the perfect boxer short. We viewed it as locating the perfect home for the family jewels. It needed to be a custom home, handmade, including a spacious ballroom with full seating and a sturdy front entrance so that no one slips out unexpectedly. This home should be built with the finest thread count Pima cotton with virtually no shrinkage (on our part).

So behold, we present you the Royal Highnies, the only place that deserves to house the family jewels."

Shrinkage aside, Ron's a class act. And if you want a pair, they cost a mere $79!

Our three new team members duly arrived at about 11.00pm last night after a five-hour drive from Orlando. Jeremy is a former Olympic windsurfer as well as a keen cyclist, and century rides are a cruise for him. Brannon hadn't done one yet, but I was sure he would be OK. Marcus was their entertaining support driver. I met Brannon and Marcus in Burundi last year and then flew down to Orlando to speak at a number of meetings Brannon organized just a few months back. We went to the Waffle House for an early breakfast and then all the team regrouped at the departure point. I'm not sure what it is about Marianna mosquitoes, but my bites from the previous night had turned into impressively large red welts. Craig was late back from his "family" time, but we'd let him off for that!

I spent parts of the day in a sombre mood as I received news of an apparently healthy 34-year-old friend who had died suddenly last week in England. Being on this trip I'd been out of the loop, but he died in bed next to his wife, leaving behind three precious children under the age of six. He was a fantastic man—gifted, gentle, kind and compassionate. Devastating. There are no easy answers to the big questions that such tragedies elicit, but it's a reminder of how fleeting life is. None of us knows how long we've got, so let's make sure we make it count whilst we're here. I thought of how many people were dying in Burundi right now amidst the hideous suffering (I was hearing daily reports of how much worse things were out there) and that made me all the more determined to raise as much money as possible to make an impact out there through what we're doing.

We had followed the Southern Tier ACA official route so far, but that ends at the Florida coast, whereas we wanted to finish in Charleston, South Carolina. So from Tallahassee onwards, we were going by Google Maps as we cut north eastwards. We'd had a GPS with all the ACA maps programmed in, so in theory, whenever we got lost while following the cue sheets, we could just refer to the

GPS and quickly get back on track. How would that work out now? Well, the morning went smoothly enough, although I pushed my knees too hard, so we had to collectively slow the pace a little on my account. Come Tallahassee though, it quickly became clear that it wasn't going to be so straightforward. It wasn't that big a deal, but we did get lost. It's the state capital, so a reasonably-sized city, and we ended up cycling around Florida State University for a while. Craig and Jeff would hopefully work on it later to sort out the next few days, because once out of the city, the Google Map option then directed us to a rough road that our bikes simply couldn't have coped with. Maybe the coming few days would be challenging in a different kind of way.

Outside the city we went through an area where I saw a number of young men who had bought into what objectively must be the weirdest fashion in the whole of human history. You've all seen it, I'm guessing: trousers (UK) or pants (USA) that hang not just low, revealing your underwear or builder's bum, but below the butt completely!

So I'm watching this guy walking along the road with his hands in his pockets, his jeans starting at his knees, totally revealing his blue boxers in full (they're nice enough, I suppose), but then every five steps he hoists his jeans up, only for them to drop back down to his knees again! Am I just really old and decrepit or is that the most bizarre sartorial trend ever? Do they know how stupid it looks? Should I tell them? Do they want to know? So many questions, but likewise so many mysteries in life! I remember observing a street fight once, with two lads punching each other. They'd both bought into this trend as well, so were swinging punches in between pulling up their trousers/pants, and then one of them literally fell over because his trousers had slipped too low and he'd got his legs all in a twist. Hi-la-rious! I later came across this article:

"A judge in Prattville, Alabama, sent a man to prison for three days because his trousers were hanging too low. LaMarcus Ramsey, 20, was in court charged with handling stolen goods when Judge John Bush took exception to his jeans. "You are in contempt of court because you showed your butt," he ruled. "When you get out you can buy pants that fit, or at least get a belt."

We'd covered 84 miles by late lunch, but had lost an hour with changing time zones. At last we were in the same time zone as Lizzie, which meant we must be nearly home. So after scoffing down some good nosh prepared by John (who was surprising even himself, I think, with his culinary skills), we got back on the road for a short stint to the finish. But as soon as we mounted our bikes, a thunder storm kicked in. It had been brutally hot (for us pale-skinned Brits at least) until then, but suddenly there was a sharp drop in temperature, large, heavy rain drops pelted down on us, and there was a bit of thunder and lightning. Jeff was our man with the GoPro camera which he stuck on his helmet, so during storms we trusted that if lightning struck, he'd take a hit for the team! The whole situation wasn't ideal at all as we were on a main road without a cycling lane, with 18-wheelers careering past us just a few feet away, spraying water in our faces and blowing us sideways. Thankfully, it didn't last long. We finished off 104 miles and headed back to Tallahassee for an evening with new hosts.

∞ DAY 31 ∞
PRIORITIES

Last night our hosts were David and Valerie and their two daughters, Sydney (20) and Connie (18). The girls were immediately swooning over our accents and sat down to listen to us, not for the content but just the sound! It's funny, the number of times I've given talks around the States and afterwards someone has said: "Thanks for your talk, I love your accent!" Damned with faint praise if that's all that stuck! Actually, an American friend of mine once said that my accent was worth an extra twenty IQ points in terms of how intelligent people would perceive me to be—which is useful because I need all the help I can get!

The whole evening was great fun. They were superb hosts. Valerie worked for the State Governor. US politics is so fascinating to me and wherever we have been cycling throughout this enormous nation, we have been bombarded with campaign signs or billboards saying: "Vote for Hugh Jass for Sheriff" or "Ivor Biggun for District Commissioner", etc. (Incidentally, Ima Hogg was the real name of a Texas governor's daughter!) There are insane amounts of money spent in political campaigning here, which if successful leads to so much power. So the current Governor spent—wait for it—$60 million of his own money to get elected to a position that pays $130,000 per year. His name's Rick Scott and, as Marcus noted, "Never trust a man with two first names!"

David was a state trooper for years, working the Florida Turnpike between Miami and Ft. Pierce, one of the heaviest drug-smuggling areas in the country. So he had all sorts of stories to tell: getting shot at, stopping a car with 950kg of cocaine in it as well as a gun used to murder someone the day before, all sorts of stuff. He said when he was young, it was "fun and gun", he loved it, but once he had a family, the reality of potentially dying meant he needed to get out of the game. In a strange way I could relate to that with working in Burundi. Not that I'll stop taking risks out there, but having family certainly makes me more measured in decision-making. My bottom line is choosing not to take decisions from a paradigm of fear (as most people do), but rather from faith. David now works for the

State Department doing some very interesting stuff which he'd prefer I didn't write about. Shame! It was nice to have a positive interaction with someone from the State Department after all our very negative experiences with them, being delayed for a year whilst trying to get a visa to enter the country. So up until today, if I'd played the game "word association" with you, State Department would have immediately brought to mind "bureaucratic fascists" and such like! Sorry David, as is always the case, don't judge individuals by their organization.

Valerie actually took the day off work so she could fix us breakfast, far earlier than she would have liked! She and David sent us off with bloated stomachs and contented spirits. Actually, over breakfast Jeremy looked at how much Jeff and I were chomping through and made the observation: "My theory is that you guys are creatures of habit. In that first difficult week in the mountains where you had to burn 6,000 calories a day to get over those humps, you got used to stuffing your faces, and you just never stopped, even when the mountains ended and you no longer needed so much fuel." He may well have been right because Jeff had put on 8lbs during the trip. My metabolism meant that no matter what I ate, I remained a skinny runt. Craig was definitely a bit of a porker though, and I mean that affectionately and non-judgmentally of course!

We said our goodbyes and headed off to our starting point. In the Honey Badger, I was lying down reading in the rear as I normally do, when Ron came back with tears in his eyes. He was having an amazing time on this ride. It was potentially really life-shaping for him. He loves his family so much and wanted to get things in the right order in life. We talked about how screwed up people's priorities are—how so many work so hard to live beyond their means, spending money they don't have on things they don't need to impress people they don't like, sacrificing their loved ones in the process. That's here in the affluent West at least, and particularly where we are in Mount Pleasant. Most people still aren't happy. They just have more money to spend on disguising and masking their hurts and hang-ups. Along the same theme, a number of people asked Craig how on earth he could take thirty-five days off from work. "It's easy," he said, "it's just a question of priorities. I made this adventure a priority. If you prioritized it, you could do it too." And he's no slacker, let me tell you. He's worked like a dog for the last fifteen years. So maybe there's a challenge in there for some of us? It's not about doing what we've done, it doesn't have to be that long or physically taxing—but prioritize something that has more significance to it than the big buck and move from success to significance. After all, nobody on their death bed ever regretted spending less time at the office...

Today we ended our run of fifteen consecutive century rides. We could have done one, but it would have meant cycling further and further away from our host family for the evening, so just before we set off, we decided to do a mere 75 miles, which still meant driving 40 miles back (it's a matter of saving money, because the Honey Badger guzzles so much, averaging about 7 miles to the gallon). We're so fit now that 75 miles feels like a recovery ride or a rest day. We cruised along, entering Georgia (our ninth state) very early on.

A treat came as we were about to stop for lunch when a car went by with some familiar, but out-of-context, faces in it. Bob and Lynn Lawrence, with their son Newman and his wife Trish were returning from a family holiday, and so they stopped off for a lovely bonus lunchtime chat. Burundi has deeply impacted them as a family. Bob returned from his first visit and used to sing a Kirundi song each morning to Lynn when they woke up. Newman and younger brother Will Henry both went out and were very affected, and now Newman and Trish are heading out for two years to work in Uganda. I love how Burundi blows people away beautifully and has a unique impact on those who experience it.

We finished early and headed back to Valdosta to a business friend of Ron's called Brian. His wife Chris greeted us and was shocked because she'd been expecting nine Africans—that's what Brian had told her—but we were all very definitely Caucasian! They had this humongous property and I was ensconced in the pool house. We enjoyed their hot tub and I beat up Ron in the pool as punishment for the transparent boxers episode.

Craig's family swung by to pick him up for another night away. Of course, he had valid reasons for wanting to go off with them, but would also have enjoyed staying to enjoy the plush comforts. Little Joel was ecstatic with wonder as he recounted their visit to the zoo, during which he'd been allowed to hold a baby crocodile briefly which had urinated on him. I love that sense of undiluted wonder in kids that so easily gets lost in us older ones as the years fly by. There is so much to hold in awe as we go about our lives, not just on a cycling trip, if we have eyes to see and make time for it.

We finished with an amazing BBQ supper—a few more thousand calories to add to the bank—and the evening culminated in John and David embracing a $100 wager (by the Florida boys) to swim across the snake-infested lake. John took the prize, gallantly shared $20 of the spoils, and instead of a winner's floral garland he picked up some nice green algae along the way. I'm glad the snakes didn't surface, because we were debating who was more expendable. John was the only one who could drive the Honey Badger, so was pretty crucial to our cause and David was going to produce an amazing documentary, so was likewise integral. Who would you have prioritized? And more importantly, referring back to earlier, on more significant issues, who and what are you prioritizing in life…?

CHAPTER EIGHT

RISING ELATION

∞ DAY 32 ∞

STOPPED BY POLICE, NUDITY ISSUES,
CLOSE SHAVES AND 130 MILES!

We were up at 6.00am for a great breakfast prepared by Chris. My neck was sore from fighting Ron in the pool yesterday, so maybe I didn't get the better of him as I'd thought. As we ate, Brian talked about Northerners coming down and taking some of his business with obscenely low contract bids. He's an airport runways contractor. Ron said, "Well, they must be cleverer than us to be able to do things so cheaply." Brian replied, "We know those damn Yankees are cleverer than us because they keep telling us they are!" There's undeniably a huge amount of condescension frequently shown by Northerners towards Southerners, the former considering themselves more enlightened and sophisticated compared to the latter whom they characterize as backward and quaint.

As with England, there's a North-South divide, though here of course it arises historically out of a huge amount of bloodshed. It just so happens that last night I read on the BBC's website about new estimates regarding the numbers of people who died during the American Civil War (1861-65). About 750,000 people are reckoned to have died during those years, which would translate into about 7.5 million US deaths in proportion to America's current population. In proportion to Britain's 2010 population of 62.3 million, it would equate to about 1.5 million people. So it was a deeply traumatic time in this nation's history and it's a victory, in a sense, that people aren't killing each other any more, just making jokes about each other. I witnessed plenty of prejudice both ways in my encounters over here, but one thing I can say from our experiences over this month is that we've been undeniably blessed as recipients of the famous "Southern hospitality". Our hosts everywhere have really known how to treat guests well.

So off we headed. Craig met us back at the Honey Badger having had his third cheeky night in a row away from the team, spent with his belle. They had been stopped by the police in their car this morning before the rising of the sun, no doubt because they looked like guilty students returning to campus after some elicit nookie—or maybe it was his latex cycling mankini that drew the policemen's attention. At any rate, the cops seemed satisfied by Craig's crazy explanation that he was cycling across the US in thirty days with a bunch of other guys, but had just been off for a night with his family—not sure I would have believed him!

We began cycling, not knowing how far we'd go today. There was a festive atmosphere as we were nearing the end of this mammoth ride. I think our tyres were sensing the imminent ending too, because mine gave up the ghost yesterday and Jeff's did today. We actually had six punctures between us, which obviously took a fair bit of time to fix in total. Jeremy had one puncture which could have ended badly as his tyre connected with a Matchbox dinky toy abandoned in the road. The tyre popped, he lost some control on what was a very busy road, but managed to pull off away from the traffic after initially heading towards them.

We spent mile after mile on Highway 84, which was dead flat for the most part. Sometimes there was only an eighteen inch cycling lane, with the occasional twig or road kill rending the ride all the more dangerous as big trucks steamed past us. We saw signs for Augusta, where the Golf Masters kicked off today, which is one of Georgia's main claims to fame. Speaking about golf, Winston Churchill once said, "It is an ineffectual attempt to direct an uncontrollable sphere into an inaccessible hole with instruments ill-adapted to the purpose!"

By the time we hit the 82-mile mark, we needed to leave Highway 84 and follow Google Maps to the next road. But after a few miles, we realized that Google Maps were no good to us, because they led us to a sandy path that our bikes simply couldn't handle, so we had to backtrack five miles. Then some more punctures followed, so we lost our speedy momentum and took a lunch break.

Last night I read about Levi Leipheimer, the USA's top cyclist, who was training in Spain this week when a car smashed into him. He was in the cycling lane minding his own business on a four lane road and an old driver careered into him at 80km per hour. Levi's obviously now out of action, but thought he would die, so was grateful to still be alive.

As we cycled further throughout the afternoon, the roads became busier and busier, and frankly more and more dangerous. You know things are serious when the odd obnoxious driver swerves towards you to make a point that you shouldn't be there. We had a few close shaves in the mix. I was thinking about what happened to Leipheimer and feeling a heavy sense of responsibility, imagining how hideous it would be if anything happened to one of us—all the more knowing that they wouldn't have been here if it's wasn't for me.

By this stage we'd gone past a hundred miles and our Florida friends had more than a five-hour drive back to Orlando, so we said goodbye to them and they headed off home. It was great to have them with us for the last three days. Brannon particularly left his mark (and then reinforced it repeatedly) with his staggeringly regular trips to the bathroom, which he assured us was business as usual.

We were nearing Savannah. Knowing that the next day's weather wasn't looking good and that the roads we were using were not the safest on this last leg to Charleston, we wanted to get through as many miles today as possible. So we ploughed on for what ended up being 130 miles in total. We had originally intended to find an RV park, but had contacted an old friend whom I'd met in dramatic fashion last year and, at just forty five minutes' notice, she'd invited us to her place in Bluffton. How I first met her is worth retelling:

Last June, I'd driven down from Charleston to Bluffton to give a few talks over the weekend. On the Saturday night I spoke to a youth group, after which I was dropped off at this beautiful house where I would be staying. The owner was out of town, but the annex was open, and I was told I should make myself at home. I'm an extreme extrovert, so I remember feeling disappointed that I'd not have anyone to be with all evening. I always prefer to stay with a family than in a hotel, as I love meeting new people.

There was a swimming pool out the back, but I didn't have any swimwear with me so I just jumped in naked. On my 22nd length I looked up to see a very shocked lady walking towards me, asking who on earth I was! I was in "Bluff" in the buff! So I bared my all, body and later soul, and our friendship went deep very quickly during the course of the rest of the evening! So this was my second evening with Joanie and, I promise you, I had clothes on all the way! We had a lovely supper with her, Cheryl and Kim, and then it was time for bed.

∞ DAY 33 ∞

METHANE EMISSIONS BY COWS AND DAUGHTERS

We allowed ourselves a lie-in until 7.30am this morning, as we only had a short ride. We were well ahead of our planned mileage and, in fact, could have made it all the way back to Charleston today at a stretch (c.130 miles) but we had cool hosts planned for the evening and I was due to give a talk, so it wasn't really an option anyway. We clicked on the weather forecast at breakfast and it talked of thunderstorms, flood risks, and all sorts, so we braced ourselves for an unpleasant few miles. Joanie sent us off with much better instructions regarding which roads to use, which doubtless saved us a lot of hassle.

We had to drive from Bluffton SC, where we'd spent the night, back into Savannah, Georgia, to then re-enter South Carolina legitimately on our bikes. This was our tenth and final state. It was cold, miserably cold, thirty degrees cooler than yesterday. We had a headwind blowing at us. Our spare bike was not properly attached on the back of the Honey Badger and fell off resulting in serious damage and I hoped it would not prove to be a costly mistake for our last full day tomorrow. I'd put away all my cold-weather clothing two weeks ago, but it was really needed. Everyone felt it, apart from Craig, for whom it was normal English cycling weather. The rest of us had only been used to cycling in blazing sunshine and humidity, apart from the early days of this adventure when we were up in the mountains.

Ron continued to crack me up. I speak BBC English, whereas he speaks Southern English—if that is a real term. It essentially meant that he understood one in three words that I said and was constantly asking me to repeat myself. To explain his struggles to understand me, he said with his slow gentle voice, "Mah father married mah sister, but didn't affect me none!" As we entered South Carolina the sign read, "Welcome to South Carolina—Smiling Faces, Beautiful Places." Ron mentioned a lawyer friend of his upstate who had a divorce case to deal with. His client asked him in deadly earnest, "Now look, I just need to know something: if my wife and I get divorced, will she still be my cousin?" Oh dear, I guess I'm providing legitimate ammunition for the Yankees against Southerners divide!

Discussing the previous night's gorgeous, fat, juicy steaks, Craig was expounding the environmental damage in terms of methane emissions, water usage to feed cows, grain consumed by cows, etc. "You could kill world hunger by the Western world cutting out meat once a week," he insisted. I'm not doing him justice here, because his words were very coherent, the argument cogent; it was vegetarian evangelism par excellence. But he got short shrift from Ron: "Oh, just go and eat a handful of grain and leave me alone!"

Aargh, the riding was miserable. We had four punctures within the first 29 miles. We pressed on along Alligator Alley, hoping to see one of them and maybe catch one to provide as a pet to my littl'uns tomorrow! Jeff, now truly on his home-turf in terms of bird knowledge, saw a beautiful one flutter by. As usual I kept my mouth shut to avoid confirming my ornithological ignorance, because I would have said it was a penguin or a puffin, but he chimed with great authority: "That's a pileated woodpecker with its red mohawk!"

He then explained to us what all South Carolinians know—but not necessarily many other people—about the Palmetto palm tree which is on the State flag. Unlike other trees, whose trunks are mostly dead apart from the outer layers, the Palmetto's entire trunk is alive, which makes them really flexible. So during the American Revolution in 1776, when the Americans eventually kicked our

British butts all the way back to Blighty, Fort Moultrie on Sullivan's Island was made from Palmettos as they effectively acted like shock absorbers when the Brits fired cannon balls against her. Unlike regular trees or bricks, which would have exploded upon impact, the Palmettos absorbed the full force of the cannon balls and withstood extensive damage, being so sturdy. And so the Palmetto became famous and a symbol of pride. Thanks Jeff, glad to have you on the team in more ways than one.

A lovely bunch of Bluffton folk were waiting at Parker's station to encourage us on our way. Craig's folks showed up too. So we had lunch, feeling very weary, windswept and cold. It went down as our least enjoyable stint on the road, counting down the miles until we reached Beaufort. A one-mile stretch over a bridge across the water was memorable in terms of how exhausted we were as we pounded into the gale.

Bill and Cindy were our delightful hosts for today, whom I'd met a few times over the last couple of years. We got to them at 4.00pm. Strangely we were at least as tired as on other days when we'd cycled twice as long because of the sapping wind that buffeted us all over the place for several hours. I fell asleep on the floor before a load of their friends arrived for a lovely evening with food and a talk by yours truly.

Later I spoke to Lizzie and was counting down the twenty hours until I could hold and kiss her again after thirty-five days apart. I couldn't wait! She told me how Grace (4), when having her goodnight chat and cuddle in bed this evening, made a circle on her tummy and said, "Mummy… are farts round?" That kind of searching and inquisitive mind fills me with pride and hope for future generations of Guillebauds! My all-time favourite from her was when she was in her swimsuit a while back. She clenched her lower cheeks together and said, "Look Mummy, my bottom can hug itself!"

∞ Day 34 ∞

Superheroes and Delusions of Grandeur!

I fell asleep on the sofa last night and woke up cold at 3.00am, so it was another bad night's sleep. At 6.00am Brent and John showed up from Charleston to join us on our last leg and there was also Matt who came last night. They brought superhero costumes with them, so today I was Superman, Craig was Spiderman, Jeff was Captain America, John was Batman and David was his sidekick, Robin. Our host Bill nipped out before 7.00am to bring us piping hot, fresh bagels straight from the oven and then we were off.

We headed back to Wal-Mart which was our starting point. David filmed us and did a photo shoot in our new garb as we got the bikes checked over and tyres pumped up. But then the Security Officer showed up in his wannabe police car. The poor guy was trembling, sweating and pale-faced as he circled twice, reported back to his superiors by radio and then bravely plucked up the courage to confront us five superheroes with our crime. He wound down the window and I leant in. It smelled like he had already peed himself. I thought of using my laser eyes to intimidate him, but he was already putty in my hands. It's nice to just exude authority by your presence. Maybe I would wear my cape a bit more often (although it provided more drag than lift as I rode). He bleated some high-pitched blurb about Wal-Mart not allowing photo shoots and then wheeled pitifully away with his tail between his legs. Only then did I remember that I was meant to be a superhero rather than a villain, but wow, I tell you, it felt good!

We didn't have many miles to complete today, so we took it easy, with long breaks. Actually it was very cold at the start with full extra clothing needed, but the sun soon pierced through to provide the perfect weather for the climax to the ride. Unfortunately, the only route up to Charleston was Highway 17, which is a very busy road, so we needed to be vigilant all the way. Brent and John got separated from us at one stage, but we hooked up again by lunch. By that stage we had passed the 3,000-mile mark for the trip. It was funny because you forget you're dressed as a superhero and people were staring at us as we behaved completely normally! Similarly, in Burundi I get stared at the whole time and in some ways people likewise think I can solve all their problems, just because I'm white. I think overall I prefer to be regular Simon, neither a superhero nor a standout because of my skin colour.

A few ladies saw our sign as we were parked up, googled it, and then knocked on our door to give us a donation. One of them saw Jeff's outfit and said incredulously, "Are you wearing a cape?" He explained we all were dressed as superheroes, but then looked around and he was the only one still wearing his outfit! They obviously thought he was a little odd, but still made a donation! Then another lady approached us and gave two donations—one towards the orphanage and one, she insisted, for a pitcher of beer for us—at least I trust that's what she meant, rather than beer for the orphans because that's not how we go about training them to be Burundi's future shapers and shakers! Those two encounters were just a typical sign of being back in Charleston, recently cited by Times magazine as the city with the friendliest people in America.

As we cycled the last stretch I bombed ahead, similar to Craig a few days ago as he desperately wanted to see his family again. My speedometer melted as my superlegs rotated at a cadence never seen before. I was on a mission. I began sporadically screaming or whooping with delight. The realization hit home that we'd actually made it. After one such whoop Jeff asked, "Is that your mating cry?!" No, it was sheer elation, joy and relief. I'd spent months injured before the trip and I never thought this day would come. But then, after one such spontaneous cry of happiness, in the next breath I burst into tears—tears of sadness for old Geoff, the instigator of Bike for Burundi, who was still suffering back in England right now. His ordeal was on-going. He'd sent messages of encouragement to us several times daily. I knew how totally devastating this episode had been to him, even though he'd taken it on the chin like the tough nut he is. He's such a precious friend and today's experience to me felt incomplete without him. I don't think the others had any idea that I was crying, as I was out at the front, except that my nose started pouring with snot, so I cleared it summarily, as is standard cycling practice. What is also standard etiquette, however, is to make sure nobody's right behind you to receive it in their face. But I didn't care at that stage and duly heard Craig cry, "Yuck, Simon!" Sorry buddy, I did it for Geoff!

I actually now wished we'd worn these outfits every day of the ride. They just brought out the best in folk. People everywhere cheered us on, put their hands out of their car windows to give us a high five, called out to us, laughed at us. It was such a joyous atmosphere. In the city, a few groups of folk recognized us and squealed with glee. Some friends along the way were waiting for us and had banners welcoming us home. One friend of Jeff's was on his bike and joined us for the last few miles. Ron provided great entertainment at a traffic light when he literally fell completely sideways to the ground, still strapped into his cleats. Maybe the English contingent found it all the more funny as he'd been telling us as we cycled through the historic parts of town, "This is where we kicked the Brits out… this is where the Brits got hammered by us…" etc.

There was a fabulous greeting party waiting for us at our home. Lizzie, the kids, a few neighbours, other wives and family members, gave us a great welcome. I can't tell you how wonderful it was to hold Lizzie, Zac, Grace and Josiah in my arms and kiss them many times over. It had been costly to them to be without husband/Daddy all this time and I didn't take that for granted at all. Lizzie and co had prepared a gorgeous spread. We chomped away, caught up with loved ones, had a few speeches, and the kids enjoyed playing in the Honey Badger. Then it was time to unpack all our gear, food supplies etc out of the Honey Badger in preparation for the last symbolic stretch tomorrow to dip our tyres in the Atlantic Ocean on Easter Sunday with several dozen others.

I felt emotionally and physically spent. It was time for sleep, at last back in my own bed, in my own home, with my own wife (just staying with the "owns" there, but be assured, she's the only wife I ever plan to be with!). I'd offered her my honour and she was about to honour my offer. However depleted the energy stocks may be, there's always a little left in the tank for that!

∞ DAY 35 ∞
GAME OVER!

It was such a pleasure to wake up back in my own bed with a "lie-in" until 6.34am when Josiah (2) woke up. Things had changed in my absence. He no longer wore nappies/diapers at night and he said totally unprompted, "Can I share one of my Easter eggs with the orphans?", which I hoped was a sign of a future man of compassion and generosity. One less positive development was that he now says "wadder" instead of "water", which is slightly disconcerting. I'd have to thrash that accent out of him before it became too entrenched (oh dear, that's the third prejudice I've revealed—what a bigot I am!)

It was a frenetic early morning of going to pick up bread from the bakery, getting all the kids ready, as well as a picnic together for thirty people, and then climbing into the Honey Badger to head off to Boone Hall Plantation for the beautiful St Andrew's Easter service. Each year they put up a huge marquee which seats 4,000 people and that was always the focus for us on our ride—the climax of Bike for Burundi. The weather was cool but sunny, everyone was spruced up, and it was fun to meet up again with so many people who had been supporting and following us over the last five weeks. It was slightly disconcerting actually, bearing in mind how transparent I'd been on my blog, to be talking to people knowing that they knew wa-a-a-y too much about me, the state of my backside, what I had done last night etc! My buddy Mark looked behind my back and said, "Just checking your fanny's still there!" That's been one of the bonus joys of this trip: the mix of US and UK dynamics, with all their attendant misunderstandings and discoveries.

There was a long line of people waiting for the temporary toilets and I stood in line as everyone else did. But Jeff was not yet used to being back in civilization, so he just peed in the bushes amidst thousands of guests. Jeff, those days are gone now, from hereon in please use regular facilities like the rest of the developed world! We had a lovely picnic and then slowly mobilized about twenty-five of us to do the last 6 miles to the Isle of Palms.

We wended our way across the bridge and to the beach before carrying our bikes along the sand and dipping them in the Atlantic Ocean, thirty-four days after doing the same in the Pacific Ocean. We each had a bottle of champagne and sprayed them everywhere like Formula One winners, before jumping into the water and hugging each other. Precious times. The end had come. We could have done this yesterday, but it was nice to be with a whole bunch of others to share the experience.

Why finish today? Because Easter is such a significant day. Without Easter I wouldn't be working in Burundi. Without Easter, there would be no hope. The history of humanity swung on the fact that about two thousand years ago, a closely-guarded tomb lay empty. The authorities, both Roman and Jewish, tried to explain it away, but nobody to this day has been able to give a coherent explanation other than that Jesus rose from the dead and suddenly a scared ragtag bunch of eclectic folk became emboldened to travel far and wide sharing, at great personal cost, about this extraordinary event.

I think back to Arizona, a month ago to the day. I was cycling along, in pain, feeling discouraged with my head down. The others further back shouted at me to raise my eyes. I looked up to see the name of the town we were entering: Hope! Once through the other side, another sign greeted us: Beyond Hope! But the original Easter events mean that we're never beyond hope, because death was overcome by the One who said that He had come to take our mess and die in our place. He died so that we can live—live fully in this life and then into eternity. That's the Easter message, if you didn't know it.

There was a crazy old pioneer in ancient times called Paul whose sudden transformation gave us the term "Damascus-road experience". Initially he saw it as his job to wipe out this new-fangled cult, but then he got blitzed and spent the rest of his life spreading the good news. He suffered a lot, and there's an episode he recounts where he's wrestling with a "thorn of the flesh"—be it sickness or whatever—that he just can't shake off. He says that he asked God three times to take it away from him, but eventually got this answer from God: "No, my grace is sufficient for you, for my power is made perfect in weakness." So Paul goes on: "Therefore I will boast all the more gladly about my weaknesses, so that Christ's power may rest on me."

What am I on about? Well, three days before I was due to fly out to LA to begin Bike for Burundi, I tried fifteen minutes on the cycling machine in the gym, after four months of injury, and gave up. My knees couldn't take it. I was totally discouraged and weighed down. We'd spent so many hours of planning, preparing, emailing folk etc, and I was going to crash out on day one with weak, injured knees. However, my incredible physical therapist, Jill, reassured me, "Simon, you can do it! This is perfect. If you weren't injured, you could take all the credit and plaudits at the end for yourself. As it is, when you complete the ride, it'll have to be God who gets the glory because your knees are just so weak."

So there you have it. What I didn't tell you throughout this journey was that I tried to pray every single mile of the trip: "Lord, this is for your glory." Of course, I sometimes forgot, and might have gone dozens of miles without praying it. But then a shooting pain would quickly get me back to that prayer. "Every mile for your glory, Lord!" And Jill was right! I did make it. I couldn't believe it. It was an amazing feat. But plenty of people had accomplished it before us and would do after us. The amazing thing for me was that my knees were shot and I shouldn't have made it, but somehow I did. And for that reason, with Paul, I will boast all the more gladly about my weaknesses, so that Christ's power may rest on me. He's the reason we embarked on all this. He made himself ultimately weak on the cross, to the death, so that we might be raised up with him in his resurrection. Wow! If you don't get it, then just check out what Easter is all about. Give it a really good look. Feel free to ask me any questions, or someone you know whose life reflects the beauty of an amazing God. Or check out www.alpha.org. And may the empty tomb with the stone rolled away rock your world as it has mine!

All good things come to an end, so they say, although the ramifications of Easter defy that cliché. But in the case of this book it's true! I've enjoyed it. I hope you have. Now put the book down, grab hold of your life and live it! Over and out!

EPILOGUE

A month after the ride little had changed. My knees were still giving me grief and I just hoped that with disciplined strengthening exercises, I wouldn't suffer long-term damage. I couldn't seem to stop eating ridiculous quantities of food, which was the biggest tension in our largely wonderful marriage, because Lizzie thought I was just being a glutton. Jeff was currently languishing in custody for continuing to pee in public places after repeated warnings not to. Craig had embarked on a lucrative tour of satellite TV chat-shows in Eastern Europe with his mother after the incredible revelations made earlier on our journey that he actually goes to the bathroom to break wind. That news went viral, believe it or not—it just blows viewers away, as it did me—but the Craig and Lynn tag-team now have a "How to bring up a squeaky (smelling) clean son" DVD and book series is in the pipeline. John had flown back to his home in California and was struggling with feelings of inadequacy at the size of his own engine post-Honey-Badger-driving. David was feverishly working on the documentary of our trip to get it out in good time. Geoff was slowly recovering back in England.

Of the six of us, only David had a steady job and was the only one seemingly not in transition. Jeff was heading out to Burundi to volunteer for a year or so. Craig had sold his business to do the ride and was now working for the people he sold up to. John's and Geoff's plans were very much up in the air, and the Guillebaud clan were packing up ready to head back to Africa after our two-year stint in South Carolina. It had been a fun time, but new challenges awaited us in that most difficult of places, my beloved Burundi.

$304,000 has been raised at the time of writing, but it'll be more by the time you're reading this, as $10+ per book goes to the pygmy and orphan work. So please, buy a whole load more from www.bikeforburundi.com, *and get the beautiful feature-length DVD documentary as well,* for birthday or Christmas presents for your loved ones, so that we can impact even more lives.

A number of people wanted to know why on earth we are so committed to working in such a dangerous country. To read a very different but no less fascinating account, I'd encourage you to get hold of my previous book *Dangerously Alive* (details below). I'll take one extract from it to give you a taster and also to answer the above question:

It was August 1998 and I had recently finished living in the East End of London whilst doing some theological training. Over the last year my constant prayer had been, "God, I trust you. I'll do anything, I'll go anywhere. Just make it clear." As my course had gradually come to an end, I had seen my contemporaries beginning to get jobs lined up. It was now the last week and I was still clueless as to what would happen next. My prayer became more frustrated than ever: "Lord, please! I'm twenty-five, single, available, have no ties and I'm willing to go anywhere and do anything. I beg you, reveal your purposes for my life!"

Later that day someone passed me a note with a name and telephone number scribbled on it. A man had been trying to track me down. I rang him and we arranged to meet the next day. Was the answer about to come? We met in central London. After introducing himself, he told me, "Simon, I've been praying, and I believe God's sent me to you. How would you feel about working in Burundi?"

My heart began beating faster. I asked him to tell me more, and he explained to me about the great needs among the youth in Burundi and how the church there was desperate for trained personnel. My mind was working overtime. I told him at the end of our meeting that I would "be spiritual and pray about it", and that I would get back to him in due course.

I began praying that if this was what God wanted me to do, He would give me a sign to confirm His will. The following Monday found me sitting at a desk in front of a computer at my old job, which my former employers had kept open for me. As I stared at the screen I wrestled with the Burundi question.

"God," I prayed silently, "if you want me to go to Burundi, please give me a sign. I know it's a hell-hole war zone, and it will mean leaving everything—family, friends, money, security—and making radical changes in my life. But, I trust you. Just give me a sign!"

It was a specific prayer request, seeking a specific answer. Just to be clear, the nation of Burundi had no connection whatsoever with my job, so yes, I was asking God to do something extraordinary. If He answered clearly, then I'd go. It would mean letting go of everything I cherished and moving to a country with a different language, climate and culture. But the bottom line for me was that this was a prayer of complete surrender. I knew that God had been challenging me to give Him command of my whole life, and to give Him permission to do with it whatever He saw fit.

But how could God possibly answer? Wasn't the demand for a sign about some obscure country in the heart of Africa a little unreasonable? Well, not long after praying, I took a phone call and a voice on the other end of the line asked me a question out of the blue which took my breath away:

"Do you know anyone who wants to work in Burundi?"

It was all I needed. This was my call. I was off...

Extract taken from *Dangerously Alive—African Adventures of Faith under Fire,* available from www.more-than-conquerors.com

ACKNOWLEDGMENTS

As you'd expect, there are lots of people who contributed to make Bike for Burundi such a success. First of all, huge thanks to the many people out there whom I can't name, who contributed sums, large or small, who prayed for us, who encouraged us and our families through some tough weeks.

Once we flew out to LA, Chris Saxton gave us an incredible start, which was a great boost at the outset. Helping Chris were his wife Jo, our hosts Katie Mello, John and Angela Schryver, Ernesto and Katrina Aldover, LCGS head honchos Bob and Pam Rognlien, and then all the riders who joined us for the first few days. Special thanks to Marshall Saville for organising it, as well as to the other riders— John Butler, Ryan Carlton, Bill Long, Samuel Victor, Doo Kang, and John Bacon; also to the cooks, Lynn and Bill Pasley, and support team, Dave Koenig and Charlie Alexovics.

Then we had a succession of amazingly generous hosts, each memorable in their different ways. Massive thanks to David and Corry Wells, Ken and Kim Burk, Chuck and Karen Gatwood, Danny and Deanna Smith, Chris and Rikki Hatter, Jeff and Darcy Gott, Liz Rogers, Michael Madison, Dan Hopper, David and Rebecca Bearden, Steve and Tania Panella, Tom and Diane Denton, David and Valerie Binder, Ken and Ceil Striplin, Robert Seawell, Brian and Chris Summers, Bill and Cindy Johnson.

The Adventure Cycling Association Southern Tier maps were a life-saver, giving us all the details we needed to get through, as well as some of the general trivia I shared on occasion. Thanks to those who put them together.

Bob McManus—you could not have known how significant would be your spontaneous act of generosity to us strangers walking past your house. Your bike became our spare that enabled us to complete the ride. Thanks so much.

Bike for Burundi would have looked very different without the Honey Badger, so thanks to Todd Gaylord for your incredible trust (John just test drove it around the block once before you allowed him to drive it all the way across America, twice!) and generosity in loaning it to us for all the time we needed it—a huge blessing.

Others who joined us along the way added great fun into the mix. Thanks to Ron Banks, Hadrian Hobbs, Brannon Rue, Jeremy Willard and Marcus Mennenga.

I'm grateful to Tim Pettingale for changing the whole blog into a book format, which wasn't as straightforward as I thought, and to Charlotte Hutchinson for some further tweaks. Also thanks to Matt Pridgen for taking on all the publishing side of things.

Our families paid a very real cost for our absence, both before and during the trip. So thanks to Michelle, Jake and Luke Morris; to Emma, Beth and Joel Riley; Ryan Strauss; and Lizzie, Zac, Grace and Josiah Guillebaud. We love you so much, and are deeply grateful to you.

And finally, the team: it was such a privilege to do this together. Old Geoff, you made it happen. Craig, thanks for being a second mother to me. Young Jeff, your enthusiasm for life is beautiful. David, you simply had a great attitude all the way. Two huge roles that deserve special mention are those played by John Stinson as driver/cook/logs man and Bonnie Turco (with Joe) as organiser. John, you had a tough job and you hung on in there, for which I'm deeply grateful. Bonnie, you bust a gut for month upon month making contacts and making sure everything would run smoothly. Great job! I'll always be thankful to you.

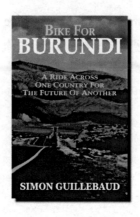

To order the feature-length documentary of our epic adventure, please go to:

www.bikeforburundi.com

If you want to sign up for the 'Tour du Burundi' as a fundraising adventure holiday of a lifetime, do get in touch with us. Burundi is sometimes called the 'Switzerland of Africa' (along with Rwanda), with all its rolling hills, so it's a beautiful and challenging cycling spot, and you'll get to see what our work involves in this amazing nation.

To find out more about the work of Great Lakes Outreach, please visit:

www.greatlakesoutreach.org

And to follow the crazy goings-on in Burundi on a regular basis, do sign up for regular blog postings at:

www.simonguillebaud.com